TELEVISION: A Guide to the Literature

by Mary Cassata and
Thomas Skill

ORYX PRESS
1985

The rare Arabian Oryx is believed to have inspired the myth of the unicorn. This desert antelope became virtually extinct in the early 1960s. At that time several groups of international conservationists arranged to have 9 animals sent to the Phoenix Zoo to be the nucleus of a captive breeding herd. Today the Oryx population is over 400 and herds have been returned to reserves in Israel, Jordan, and Oman.

Copyright © 1985 by
The Oryx Press
2214 North Central at Encanto
Phoenix, Arizona 85004-1483

Published simultaneously in Canada

Printed and Bound in the United States of America

∞ The paper used in this publication meets the minimum requirements of American National Standard for Information Science—Permanence of Paper for Printed Library Materials, ANSI Z39.48, 1984.

Library of Congress Cataloging in Publication Data

Cassata, Mary B., 1930–
   Television, a guide to the literature.

   Bibliography: p.
   Includes index
   1. Television broadcasting—Bibliography.   I. Skill,
Thomas.   II. Title.
Z7711.C37   1985   [PN1992.5]   016.38455   83-43236
ISBN 0-89774-140-4

For Jay Martin Poole
Who, from the beginning, encouraged us to
undertake this project and gave us the
moral support to carry it through to
completion—even though, in the process,
there were times when we felt like cursing
rather than blessing him.

Table of Contents

Acknowledgements

We wish to thank the following persons at our respective universities whose assistance have made this work possible:

From SUNY/Buffalo: Christa Mauro for her dogged persistence in tracking down many of the entries; Marcy Haimowitz for her assistance in verifying and typing chapter bibliographies; and Patty Rackl for her extraordinary efforts in deciphering the poor penmanship and for typing and proofreading many of the chapters.

From the University of Dayton: Dr. James D. Robinson for his helpful critiques of the chapter drafts; Julie Schimpf for her assistance in the typing of chapter bibliographies; and Dr. Don B. Morlan, chairman of the Department of Communication Arts, for providing needed resources and the release time from classes.

Preface

This guide to the literature of television grew out of three bibliographic essays that we wrote originally for *Choice,* a monthly book-selection journal published by the American Library Association's College and Research Libraries division. The essays were published in the January, February, and April 1982 issues. From the beginning, the project proved to be an ambitious one, with each book carefully selected and examined according to specific criteria established for its inclusion. We divided the literature of television into three broad categories: "Test Patterns," "The Environment," and "Directions." These categories proved to be such a good fit for our original essays that we decided to retain the same categories for this volume, for which we greatly reworked and expanded the original essays. Thus, Part I, "Test Patterns," attempts to provide a broad overview of the communication/mass communication process, a history of television, and reference sources for information about television. Part II, entitled "The Environment," covers the research of the field, first in broad brush strokes, then in a more specialized mode, focusing on such areas as television and children, television news, and television and politics. Part III, "Directions," the concluding section, covers the literature of the television industry and television criticism and ends with a number of thought-provoking collected works.

Mary Cassata and Thomas Skill

Part I
Test Patterns

Introduction

It seems hard to believe that scarcely more than 35 years ago a Gallup poll was asking: "Do you know what television is?" "Have you ever seen a television set in operation?" Today, no one would dare dispute either that, for better or worse, television has changed the quality of our lives or that we have been its willing abettors. Few can remain neutral to the question of what television really is. Depending upon our moods and needs, this electronic member of the family is at times a magic carpet, escape hatch, or rut; a window on the world, mirror, or stone wall; a tranquilizer or stimulant; a relief or irritant; a friend or stranger; an entertainer or teacher; a companion or antagonist; a guest or intruder; a time-passer or time-waster.

Few can escape its presence. It is firmly ensconced in 98 percent of our homes—and, in over half of them, in twos or threes or more. Its images talk and move for six and one-half hours a day in the average household. The charge has been made, and substantiated, that between the ages of 3 and 16, American children, on the average, spend one-sixth of their waking hours watching television.

When television first appeared on the American scene, it was regarded as a toy; it was hypothesized that once the novelty wore off, people would go about their daily lives as before. But, as we know, the novelty hypothesis did not hold up. Rather than decreasing, viewership has steadily risen over the years, and our lives have never been the same.

To say that television extends human perceptions beyond the reach of the unaided senses is merely giving television its due. Television has eliminated social, cultural, and economic barriers and made all of us stockholders in shared experience. Thus, in the short span of a quarter of a century, we have been participants and spectators in history brought to us by television. We have marveled at the space shots and communications from the moon. We have recoiled in horror over the John Kennedy, Martin Luther King, and Anwar Sadat assassinations and the attacks on Gerald Ford, Ronald Reagan, and the Pope. We have witnessed, right after dinner, the first televised living-room war. We have hit the campaign trail with presidential hopefuls. We were witnesses at Watergate and suffered through presidential disgrace and resignation. We were perched on an emotional seesaw for all the world to watch with the taking, holding, and releasing of the American hostages in Tehran. On the lighter side, we have all come to know Mary Richards, Archie Bunker, the Fonz, and Hawkeye, and we have laughed and cried with them.

Television has made all of us experts about what is good about it, bad about it, or indifferent about it. It has become a national pastime for all of us to talk, with conviction, about it. The millions and millions of words that have been written about television constitute a literature that examines this subject from a multiplicity of perspectives. The fact that there is a literature of television gives testimony to its impact upon the lives of the American citizenry, no matter what people say about it.

Chapter 1
Toward an Understanding of the Mass Communication Process

OVERVIEW

The literature of television cannot be fully explored without a brief identification of some of the basic publications in the more general area of communication to lay the foundation for understanding that literature. Thus, in this chapter, we look at those publications that examine the beginnings of the theoretical (and alternative) perspectives of the human communication process. Next, we explore the interdisciplinary perspectives of the mass communication process and examine their role in the development of mass communication theory. Finally, we present alternative theoretical perspectives of mass communication for some sense of the richness, depth, and complexity of the field.

COMMUNICATION PROCESSES: THEORETICAL FOUNDATIONS

One of the earliest and best known books on communication is David K. Berlo's theoretical treatise, *The Process of Communication,* written in 1960. The book explores and analyzes the communication process and investigates language and meaning. Another important pioneering effort is *The Science of Human Communication,* edited by Wilbur Schramm in 1963. This collection of essays is taken from the broadcasts of the Voice of America and includes works by many of the most prestigious researchers and theorists in communication at the time. Each essay reads like a road map to communication research as it exists today. *The Communication of Ideas,* edited by Lyman Bryson, is a seminal work which grew out of a series of lectures for a course entitled "The Problems of the Communication of Ideas." Representing the ideas and writings of such scholars as Margaret Mead, Paul Lazarsfeld, Robert Merton, Harold Lasswell, Charles Siepmann, and Robert Leigh, the book attempts to provide a diversity of routes to the study of communication: cross-cultural comparisons, ancient cultural roots, modern psychological and sociological thinking, philosophy, and technology.

Three books do an excellent job in covering the various theoretical perspectives on communication. First, Stephen Littlejohn's *Theories of Human Communication,* now in its second edition (1983), presents a concise and highly readable analysis of communication theory, which the author claims is at once "multitheoretical" and "eclectic." The book, however, is comprehensive and stands out as one of the most significant books in the field. As in the earlier edition of this work, the book is divided into five major areas. Part I serves as an introduction to the nature of communication theory. A discussion of general theories such as general systems theory, cybernetics and symbolic interactionism, and rules theory is explored in Part II. Part III discusses thematic theories—theories of language and nonverbal coding, meaning, information processing, and persuasion. Part IV is concerned with contextual theories and explores the interpersonal and mediated contexts. Finally, Part V, the author's capstone chapter, is the author's personal statement with regard to the state of the art in communication theory.

In a work similar to Littlejohn's, Werner Severin and James Tankard, Jr. offer a somewhat more introductory-level book on communication theory directed toward students in the mass media areas. *Communication Theories: Origins, Methods, Uses* presents chapters on methodology, communication models, communication context and settings, as well as communication processes and effects. Wilbur Schramm's *Men, Messages, and Media: A Look at Human Communication* offers a basic analysis of human communication in the first six chapters and then applies those fundamentals in the following eight chapters toward an exploration of mass communication. In summary, Littlejohn, Severin and Tankard, and Schramm present three works that provide substantive and readable introductions to the many theoretical perspectives on communication and should be included in basic collections in both communication and television.

In his introductory book, *Communication,* Denis McQuail approaches the field of communication from a sociological perspective. Taking a social process point of view, McQuail reviews the various models and theories of communication and summarizes relevant research in the area. A stated goal of the book is to explore how "communication processes and outcomes reflect the distribution of power in society and between societies."

For the student of communication who might wish to explore the depth and breadth of the field in greater detail, the *Handbook of Communication,* edited by Ithiel de Sola Pool, Frederick W. Frey, Wilbur Schramm, Nathan Maccoby, and Edwin B. Parker, serves as an excellent resource. While no single volume is ever complete, the *Handbook* does come close to providing a comprehensive understanding of the "state of communication knowledge" up to 1973. Its 31 essays, written by 34 communication scholars and researchers, look at communication under three broad categories: communication process, communication settings, and communication research. The work is indexed by both author and subject, and each essay has an extensive bibliography for those interested in further investigation.

COMMUNICATION PROCESSES: OTHER PERSPECTIVES

Other perspectives, coterminous with communication theory, serve as important linkages for promoting the greater understanding of the communication process. For a conceptual as well as a historical perspective on public opinion, Walter Lippmann's seminal work, *Public Opinion,* remains a classic in the field. It lays the groundwork for the origin, understanding, and analysis of public opinion and its relationship to communication.

Similarly, one of the earliest and best regarded attempts at synthesizing the extensive scholarship and research in the area of persuasion is *Communication and Persuasion* by Carl Hovland, Irving Janis, and Harold Kelley. In reporting their research on how persuasive communications affects opinions and beliefs, the authors report their findings, resulting from an extended program of primarily controlled experimental studies, as generalizations pertaining to the communicator (the who), the communication (the what), and the audience (the whom).

A discussion of the effect of communication on the development of civilizations is found in Harold Innis's *The Bias of Communication* and *Empire and Communications.* Innis defines and analyzes the communication structures of societies in terms of "time-biased" (traditional societies) or "space-biased" (contemporary societies that emphasize efficient information exchange).

Another interesting perspective is the application of rules to human behavior as presented in Susan Shimanoff's *Communication*

Rules: Theory and Research. Exploring the place of rules in axiomatic theories of communication, Shimanoff's book is regarded as an innovative and significant advance in this area of research.

In a class by itself, *Diffusion of Innovations* by Everett Rogers (third edition [1983]) returns to the title of the first edition, which was published in 1962 and shows a more than sevenfold increase over the number of diffusion publications that have appeared since then. The second edition (1971) titled *Communication of Innovations* was coauthored by F. Floyd Shoemaker. Not only bigger but better, the most recent edition presents a revision of the theoretical framework as well as the research evidence supporting the diffusion model. With the spread of diffusion studies to the developing nations, the diffusion paradigm has become more culture-free. Add to this the improved understanding of diffusion through the conveyance process and the 1983 publication emerges as another innovation milestone.

Our final selection to round out this section is the title *Communication Philosophy and the Technological Age,* edited by Michael Hyde. Consisting of five essays that address the impact of today's growing reliance on technology and the resulting impact on human communication, the authors take a phenomenological approach to their subject. The questions they ask are the difficult ones that we must all ponder as the new technologies continue to emerge, challenging the patterns of human communication and behavior.

MASS COMMUNICATION: THEORETICAL FOUNDATIONS

Several excellent publications may be considered fundamental to the study of mass communication. While examples of those that focus on psychological, economic, journalistic, historical, or other perspectives are numerous, we have found that those books using a sociological thematic approach deal with mass communication within a broader, more appropriate social and cultural framework. Three books emerge as solid examples of the sociological approach: *Theories of Mass Communication* (fourth edition), by Melvin DeFleur and Sandra Ball-Rokeach; *Mass Communication Theory: An Introduction,* by Dennis McQuail; and *Mass Communication: A Sociological Perspective,* by Charles Wright. A fourth book on communication models, *Communication Models for the Study of Mass Communication,* coauthored by Denis McQuail and Sven Windahl, might also be usefully considered with these three titles.

DeFleur and Ball-Rokeach's fourth edition retains much of the content that has made this book a classic: the interactive relationship perspective of media, society, and audience; the emergence and growth of each of the media; mass society and the beginnings of media theory; the media as social systems; the media-encountering perspectives of the audience; effects theories of television violence; media persuasion models; and an integrative model of media effects. Expanded sections concern emerging media systems, focusing on the newer technologies and the nature of human communication, with a new perspective on the biosocial theory of human communication.

By comparison, Denis McQuail's *Mass Communication Theory: An Introduction* is considered a serious competitor to the DeFleur and Ball-Rokeach book. The two are widely divergent, however, in their approach, with the latter taking a Euro-American sociological perspective. The wealth of detail covered by McQuail is a challenge even to the most experienced theories scholar; thus, it may prove overwhelming for the student with little background in the field, despite the promise of its subtitle. Because of the book's comprehensiveness, it does not cover the various perspectives in as much depth as one would like, making it necessary to consult the references McQuail uses to search out missing links. However, this may not be a criticism, for any independent intellectual stimulation such as searching out more information may reflect the true worth of this book.

McQuail and Windahl's little book, *Communication Models for the Study of Mass Communication,* might be considered a useful supplement to McQuail's theory volume. Serving the twin purposes of a historical review as well as a presentation of the most important conceptual developments in the field, this book presents numerous graphic, textual, and critical analyses of a wide variety of models which the authors categorize as basic models; personal influence, diffusion, and effects of mass communication on individuals models; models showing effects of mass communication on culture and society; audience-centered models; and mass media systems, production, selection, and flow models. The authors' commentary and bibliographic references in each of the model groupings are additional aids toward achieving an understanding of the theoretical foundations of the field.

Charles Wright's *Mass Communication: A Sociological Perspective* is out of print and needs to be updated. Nevertheless, we include it here because we consider it a basic book in the field, entirely readable and modestly unimposing. Among its strengths are the chapters addressing the functional analysis of the media; a comparative analysis of several foreign systems of mass communication with our own; and an examination of popular culture from such perspectives as the portrayal of media heroes and villains and certain minority and occupational groups.

Departing somewhat in approach from his colleagues, but nevertheless in pursuit of the same sociological grail, David Chaney organizes *Processes of Mass Communication,* around Lasswell's well-known model, "Who says What to Whom in which Channel and with What Effect?" Chaney categorizes his chapters within the broad frameworks of "Subjective Reality" (the interactive relationship between audience and content), "Objective Reality" (media organizations and technology, including production and distribution aspects), and "Meaning Performance" (content analysis and assessment aspects).

Less comprehensive than McQuail in sheer breadth of theoretical approaches presented, D.J. Crowley, in *Understanding Communication: The Signifying Web,* covers a great deal of ground in citing classic communication theory as it relates to the cultural and symbolic interaction of the Chicago School. The social and cultural contexts in which the communication process takes place are at the core of his thesis. The book covers language development, codes, symbols, and other rituals and touchstones of social reality and is recommended as an important addition to the limited number of theory books in the field.

Three titles dealing with research methodology confirm the centrality of research to the development and understanding of theory. The evidence these titles give to the resurgence of interest is especially welcome. Taking these titles in chronological order, the first is *Research Methods in Mass Communication* (1981), edited by Guido Stempel and Bruce Westley. Hailed as both a long-awaited volume and a volume worth waiting for, this comprehensive book includes the major research strategies of the field: content analysis, survey, experimental and historical research; other methodologies such as legal and qualitative research; and appropriate research designs to be applied to these methodologies. The 20 scholars, who in addition to Stempel and Westley have contributed chapters to this volume, read like a Who's Who in Mass Communication—e.g., Comstock, McCombs, Greenberg, and Carey. A final chapter, telling what to do after the research has been completed, is like putting the frosting on the cake. Next, Stempel and Westley explore the mysteries of carrying the work to full term—i.e., publication—and they explore formatting and writing styles of the journal article, dissertation, thesis, and monograph.

Arthur Asa Berger's *Media Analysis Techniques* was published in 1982 as volume 10 of the Sage CommText series. In this unimposing little book, Berger presents an exciting two-part volume, with Part One dealing with concepts and theoretical approaches and Part Two dealing with their applications. Thus, we first look at semiological, Marxist, and sociological analysis and psychoanalytic criticism. Next, we study their application in an analysis of a movie, football, fashion advertising, and all-news radio. The end result is an arresting study which clearly demonstrates that the application of different perspectives to the same content can result in vastly different interpretations.

Despite some problematical concerns, *Mass Media Research: An Introduction* (1983), by Roger Wimmer and Joseph Dominick, is another methods book, especially strong in quantitative techniques, less so in field-observation and focus-group methods, but totally lacking in legal and historical methods. However, the book, whose authors illustrate the theory/practice dichotomy, is strongest in the latter dimension with a proliferation of checklists, charts, and diagrams to help the researcher.

To conclude this section, we cite several books which are neither exclusively theoretical nor exclusively research-oriented, but which by combining elements of each, earn a place in this section. One, with the unlikely title of *Electronic Christianity: Myth or Ministry,* by Donald Oberdorfer, strongly argues the thesis of Lazarsfeld and Merton (see Bryson, *The Communication of Ideas*), which states that, in order to be effective, propaganda as disseminated by the media needs to embody one of three conditions: monopolization, canalization, or supplementation. Taking all three conditions into consideration, Oberdorfer makes the case that media ministries lack telecommunication sophistication, and he uses a still valid 1948 propaganda perspective to make his point.

The annual series, *Progress in Communication Sciences* (1979–), edited by Brenda Dervin and Melvin Voigt, integrates interdisciplinary approaches to communication research emphasizing the following areas: (1) information, information transfer, and information systems; (2) communication uses and effects; and (3) communications and information control and regulation. The purpose of the series is to assemble 8–12 diversified, state-of-the-art reviews for each volume which focus on content and coverage. Synthesis and the search for convergence is the second purpose of the series. Among the research articles in the first four volumes are the following: "Time Allocations in Mass Communication Research," by Martin P. Block (Volume 1, 1979); "Formative Evaluation of Children's Television as Mass Communication Research," by Robert LaRose (Volume 2, 1980); "The Contribution of Critical Scholarship to Television Research," by Mary Ann Heller (Volume 3, 1982); and "Semiotics and Communications Studies: Points of Contact," by Gertrude J. Robinson and William O. Shaw (Volume 4, 1984). Volumes 5 and 6 are currently in preparation.

MASS COMMUNICATION: OTHER PERSPECTIVES

A number of other perspectives of mass communication contribute to the variegated pattern and texture the field has assumed. For example, no scholar has raised the consciousness of so many people to the influence of the mass media as effectively as Marshall McLuhan. According to McLuhan's *Understanding Media: The Extensions of Man,* print engages the mind in linear ways. The electronic media, on the other hand, bombard and engage the senses in more challenging and more basic ways. Hence, his notorious aphorism: "The medium is the message," in which he argues that the interaction of mind and medium are more crucial than the content of the message and that the dominant medium of the day changes both society and culture. Unfortunately, according to McLuhan, the present has little insight into the forces that shape and mold it.

About the same time McLuhan was developing his thesis, Jacques Ellul was developing his own, which was similar to McLuhan's. His book *Technological Society* analyzes and describes the impact of technological development and change on societies as a whole. A major focus is upon what the author terms "technique," which is the "totality of methods rationally arrived at and having absolute efficiency" (p. xxv). From a sociological perspective, Ellul considers the impact of technique on social interactions, political structures, and economic phenomena.

Pulling back from technology, several books go off in different directions, examining the more social/cultural aspects of mass communication. One of the earliest examples is visionary Daniel Boorstin's *The Image,* in which he attempts to persuade his readers to come to terms with their illusions and to see through the webs of fabricated reality that encase our society. Perhaps the most important consequence of this book is Boorstin's invention of the word "pseudo-event," which has come to mean the image of everything that is unreal in our society. *Language, Image, Media,* edited by Howard Davis and Paul Walton, explores the use of language in print and electronic media in the shaping of society and the mass consciousness. Drawing upon the intellectual content of various disciplines, the 14 essays in this volume attempt to present new insights and theoretical perspectives into the role the media play in our society.

Along the same vein, but much more abstract and complex, is Stuart and Elizabeth Ewen's *Channels of Desire: Mass Images and the Shaping of the American Consciousness.* Historical, philosophical, political, and prophetical in its approach, this book plumbs both the background and the foreground that provide the necessary societal conditions for the media of mass communications to take root and develop and grow into the major forces they have become in today's society.

The final two books in this section are *Mass Entertainment* by Harold Mendelsohn and *The Play Theory of Mass Communication* by William Stephenson. In the former, the author takes a theoretical perspective in analyzing the role of mass entertainment in today's society. Penetratingly thorough, Mendelsohn attempts to present all sides of the entertainment controversy including the positive and negative arguments as well as the psychological and sociological functions of mass entertainment. In his concluding chapters, Mendelsohn makes the case for the audience's quest for quality entertainment and for the mass media to allow for the infusion of culture in mass entertainment.

Stephenson also explores the role of mass communication as entertainment. He posits the view that the play aspects of mass communication may be the way in which a society develops its culture. This view contrasts somewhat with the traditional research perspectives that see mass communication as a persuasive influence on individuals in society.

BIBLIOGRAPHY

Berger, Arthur Asa. *Media Analysis Techniques.* Beverly Hills, CA: Sage Publications, 1982.

Berlo, David Kenneth. *The Process of Communication: An Introduction to Theory and Practice.* New York: Holt, Rinehart and Winston, 1960.

Boorstin, Daniel J. *The Image: A Guide to Pseudo-Events in America.* New York: Atheneum, 1962.

Chaney, David C. *Processes of Mass Communication.* New York: Macmillan, 1972.

Crowley, D.J. *Understanding Communication: The Signifying Web.* New York: Gordon and Breach Science Publishers, 1982.

Davis, Howard, and Walton, Paul. *Language, Image, Media.* New York: St. Martin's Press, 1983.

DeFleur, Melvin L., and Ball-Rokeach, Sandra. *Theories of Mass Communication.* 4th ed. New York: Longman, 1982.

Dervin, Brenda, and Voigt, Melvin J., eds. *Progress in Communication Sciences.* Vol. 1–. Norwood, NJ: Ablex, 1979–.

Ewen, Stuart, and Ewen, Elizabeth. *Channels of Desire: Mass Images and the Shaping of American Consciousness.* New York: Mc-Graw-Hill, 1982.

Ellul, Jacques. *The Technological Society.* New York: Knopf, 1964.

Hovland, Carl Iver; Janis, Irving L.; and Kelley, Harold H. *Communication and Persuasion.* New Haven, CT: Yale University Press, 1953.

Hyde, Michael J., ed. *Communication Philosophy and the Technological Age.* University, AL: University of Alabama, 1982.

Innis, Harold Adams. *The Bias of Communication.* Toronto, ON: University of Toronto Press, 1951.

―――. *Empire and Communications.* Toronto, ON: University of Toronto Press, 1950.

Institute for Religious and Social Studies. Jewish Theological Seminary of America. *The Communication of Ideas: A Series of Addresses.* Edited by Lyman Bryson, Totowa, NJ: Cooper Square Publishers, Inc., 1948.

Lippmann, Walter. *Public Opinion.* New York: Macmillan, 1922.

Littlejohn, Stephen W. *Theories of Human Communication.* 2d ed. Belmont, CA: Wadsworth, 1983.

McLuhan, Marshall. *Understanding Media: The Extensions of Man.* New York: McGraw-Hill, 1964.

McQuail, Denis. *Communication.* New York: Longman, 1975.

―――. *Mass Communication Theory: An Introduction.* Beverly Hills, CA: Sage, 1983.

McQuail, Denis, and Windahl, Sven. *Communication Models for the Study of Mass Communication.* New York: Longman, 1982.

Mendelsohn, Harold. *Mass Entertainment.* New Haven, CT: College and University Press, 1966.

Oberdorfer, Donald. *Electronic Christianity: Myth or Ministry.* Taylor Falls, MN: John L. Brekke, 1982.

Pool, Ithiel de Sola, et al. *Handbook of Communication.* Chicago: Rand McNally, 1973.

Rogers, Everett M. *Diffusion of Innovations.* 3d ed. New York: Free Press, 1983.

Rogers, Everett M., and Shoemaker, F. Floyd. *Communication of Innovations.* 2d ed. New York: The Free Press, 1971.

Schramm, Wilbur Lang. *Men, Messages, and Media: A Look at Human Communication.* New York, Harper & Row, 1973.

Schramm, Wilbur Lang, ed. *The Science of Human Communication: New Directions and New Findings in Communication Research.* New York: Harper & Row, 1973.

Severin, Werner Joseph, and Tankard, James W. *Communication Theories: Origins, Methods, Uses.* New York: Hastings House, 1979.

Shimaroff, Susan B. *Communication Rules: Theory and Research.* Beverly Hills, CA: Sage, 1980.

Stempel, Guido H., III, and Westley, Bruce H., eds. *Research Methods in Mass Communication.* Englewood Cliffs, NJ: Prentice Hall, 1981.

Stephenson, William. *The Play Theory of Mass Communication.* Chicago: University of Chicago Press, 1967.

Wimmer, Roger D., and Dominick, Joseph. *Mass Media Research: An Introduction.* Belmont, CA: Wadsworth, 1983.

Wright, Charles Robert. *Mass Communication: A Sociological Perspective.* New York: Random House, 1959.

Chapter 2
Historical Development of Television

OVERVIEW

The medium of television did not begin its phenomenal diffusion in the United States until 1948—the same year the transistor was invented, the 33-1/3 and 45 rpm records appeared on the market, and the Kinsey Report made media headlines. At the same time, Whitaker Chambers accused Alger Hiss of transmitting documents to the Russians; a Hindu fanatic assassinated Mahatma Gandhi; and Harry S. Truman scuttled the predictions of a Thomas E. Dewey landslide in the presidential election. Were it not for World War II, television might have exploded upon the American scene even earlier, since its electronic technology had essentially been worked out in the 1920s and 1930s.

In this chapter, we look at the literature that details the broad historical milestones of the medium in both the printed word and in photographs. Then, we take a more focused look at the historical development of specific genres, hopefully reenforcing the notion that television is not a single monolithic entity but instead is made up of a number of distinctive program types or genres and should be understood as such.

HISTORICAL PERSPECTIVES

The literature on the history of broadcasting and television in the U.S. is closely associated with one individual: Erik Barnouw. Barnouw's three-volume history of broadcasting is the most important comprehensive analysis of the social, political, and legal aspects of broadcasting. Volume 1, *A Tower in Babel,* begins with Marconi's wireless in the late 1800s and extends to the 1933 broadcast of Franklin

D. Roosevelt's presidential inauguration. Volume 2, *The Golden Web,* picks up in 1933 with the development of the networks; the rise of radio's influence over American social, political, and business activities; the beginnings of television; and the personalities, both behind the scenes and on the air, who shaped and controlled the industry. This volume extends to 1953, where *The Image Empire* begins. Primarily concerned with television, this third volume traces the rapid growth of television, its impact and influence on covering and making events in America, and the collective and individual responses to the effects of the medium. Each volume of this superbly written history is richly annotated with extensive notes, indexes, bibliographies, and appendices (which include chronologies and legal documents).

In 1975, Barnouw wrote a condensed and updated single-volume work, *Tube of Plenty.* As the title indicates, this publication stresses the growth and development of television rather than the more general "broadcasting" focus found in the original three volumes. Thus, we see *Tube of Plenty* not as a single substitute for the original three-volume set, but as a continuation that focuses on the growth of television and its influence on American life.

Two works from the Arno Press collection "Dissertations in Broadcasting" take an analytical look at the DuMont television network and the historical evolution of the mass audience in broadcasting. *An Historical Study of the DuMont Television Network,* by Gary Hess, investigates the development of DuMont Laboratories in the early 1930s and traces its progression through the 1940s and 1950s until its dissolution in 1955. Hess examines the relationship between DuMont and Paramount Pictures and makes a lengthy analysis of some of the reasons for the decline of the original fourth network. *The Concept of the Mass Audience in American Broadcasting,* by Charles Stamps, traces the development of the broadcaster's concept of the audience and attempts to describe that audience at various points in broadcasting's history.

Laurence Bergreen presents an intelligent and well-documented narrative on the evolution of network broadcasting in America entitled *Look Now, Pay Later.* Bergreen analyzes the development of the network system; the people who were behind it; and how a broadcasting environment that mixes technology, commerce, and art has managed to survive and even prosper amid its past mistakes and present problems.

In *The Great Television Race,* Joseph Udelson concentrates on the television industry from 1925 to 1941, which he considers to be television's most critical formative period. Udelson combines discourses on the industry's important pioneers with analyses of the technology; economic factors; the allocation of frequencies; the competition among RCA, NBC, and CBS; and the experimental stages of public television. The book is not only generously referenced, but the author also includes a useful bibliographic essay for the reader who wishes to pursue this subject in greater depth.

A debt of great gratitude is owed to those writers of pop books on television. Taken together, such works converge into useful histories of the medium. Five books are especially notable. The first is Harry Castleman and Walter Podrazik's *Watching TV: Four Decades of American Television,* which presents a sweeping history of TV from the 1940–1941 season to the 1980–1981 season. Copiously illustrated with photographs and charts, the authors have dug deeply behind the scenes to give us a detailed, definitive work merging American popular taste with the programming that responded to those tastes and, in the process, shaped them.

Television: The First Fifty Years, by Jeff Greenfield, is a pictorial history accompanied by a well-researched text that reflects both the technological developments as well as the social, political, and programming histories. It is an oversized book with many color photographs and over 500 illustrations. *TV Book,* edited by Judy Fireman, is a compilation of articles about television from numerous perspectives by well-known TV critics, scholars, and personalities. In addition, an interspersed chronological history of television incorporates photographs and brief descriptions of selected events. *TV Guide: The First 25 Years,* edited by Jay Harris, contains 122 articles selected from *TV Guide* magazine, 1953–1977. This book covers serious times—"America's Long Vigil" (news coverage of JFK's funeral)—as well as the lighter aspects of the medium—"The Oldest Living Teenager" (Dick Clark). Finally, Max Wilk's *The Golden Age of Television* is a personal analysis of the era of television in the 1950s known as the "golden age." Wilk is sometimes sentimental about the people and programs and at other times is deadly serious (Army/McCarthy hearings). While this may not qualify as a comprehensive history of the "golden age," it does give a refreshingly different perspective on events.

An excellent anthology on the history of broadcasting is *American Broadcasting,* by Lawrence Lichty and Malachi Topping. The 93 articles included are divided into eight subject areas (Technical, Stations, Networks, Economics, Employment, Programming, Audiences, and Regulation), and a dual table of contents gives the reader the option to select readings from a chronological listing as well. Extensive notes from each article, a lengthy bibliography relevant to each of the areas, and an index are included.

Two histories of American broadcasting are outstanding: Sydney Head's *Broadcasting in America* and Christopher Sterling and John Kittross's *Stay Tuned. Broadcasting in America,* which is now in its fourth edition, has been a mainstay in American academic institutions since 1956 when the first edition was introduced. This history of radio and television has been singled out for its comprehensiveness, depth of analysis, and cross-disciplinary approach. Each edition has been updated and substantially rewritten to reflect the exponential growth in broadcasting studies. The latest edition, which is the first to be cowritten with Christopher Sterling, not only includes new materials (e.g., with regard to public broadcasting, cable, the new technologies, and recent deregulatory actions) but has been completely rewritten to enhance readability. Presenting a balanced treatment of both radio and television, this book appears to have everything from a comparative analysis of broadcasting systems worldwide to the future of broadcasting. In between are chapters tracing the growth and development of broadcasting, the noncommercial and nonbroadcast alternatives, the administrative and financial perspectives of station management, the social control of broadcasting, and the effects of broadcasting. Sterling's guide to the literature of broadcasting is a valuable bonus.

In *Stay Tuned,* authors Sterling and Kittross trace the history of broadcasting within the context of world events. An alternate table of contents presents a topical approach with such headings as Technical Innovations, Stations, Networks, Advertising, Programming, Audience, and Regulatory Trends, to name just a few. This well-written work is a valuable introduction for the new student to broadcasting history as well as a useful resource for the more sophisticated reader.

Two additional titles deserve consideration for their concise treatment. George Gordon's *The Communications Revolution: A History of the Mass Media in the United States* was undertaken as a chronological, straightforward account, covering all of the media with equal attention. The author probes the social, cultural, financial, political, economical, and technological aspects of the major media singly and interactively. The result is a valuable overview for all levels of readers. The second title, *Communication History,* by John Stevens and Hazel Garcia (volume 2 of the Sage CommText Series), is even more concise in its treatment. Instead of resorting to the traditional approaches of concentrating on media systems and personalities, the authors attempt to present a broader perspective of the field in the hope that they might suggest the interrelationships readers ought to be thinking about. The book is divided into two parts, with each of the authors taking primary responsibility for one of the parts. Garcia's Part I is devoted to redefining the discipline in terms of conceptual and historiographic problems—in addition to research problems and needs—methodology, and models for the purpose of arriving at an objective, more critical posture. Stevens, on the other hand, looks at the subject of media effects from the perspective of how public opinion influences the media and suggests other nonconventional alternatives for studying communication history.

Two books that extend our thinking along the social historical dimension are especially welcome. *Media and the American Mind: From Morse to McLuhan,* by Daniel Czitrom, takes a theoretical/philosophical approach and traces the various influences leading to the popularization of each of the media. The sociological concepts of society that serve to rationalize the context in which the media have developed are also presented. Czitrom tackles those influences conducive to the acceptance of mass communication research as a behavioral science and explores the theories and metatheories of many of the field's leading scholars. Czitrom humanizes media history by covering nearly 200 years of its intellectual and social growth.

In the second book, *American History, American Television: Interpreting the Video Past,* editor John O'Connor pulls together the views of 14 historians who examine American culture through the eyes of television and show how history and television affect each other. The fascinating aspect of this book is that these historians bring a great deal of illumination to the TV message by filling in the historical context. Through the book's unique historical perspective, we come to understand such matters as the Black bourgeoisie's objections to "Amos N' Andy;" Milton Berle's rapid popularity fadeout as television diffused into rural America; why the "You Are There" videotapes have survived; and the interaction of television and politics. A chronology of selected TV historical events, a listing of archival and manuscript sources for the study of television, a bibliography of the literature on the history of American television, and a guide to rental sources for the productions discussed in this book are valuable aids for anyone wishing to put together a syllabus outlining television history.

Although no history of television can be complete without reference to its strong roots in other media, we pause here only to note that the rapid growth and development of television was made possible only because there was easily accessible content available from other sources—from radio, soap operas and talk shows, films from Hollywood, news and information from newspapers. Hence, the older media became the content of the new medium.

TELEVISION GENRES

In addition to their contribution to the history of the TV medium, specific histories of program genres also serve to remind us that television is not the monolithic entity so many of the medium's critics believe it to be. By concentrating on a single genre, such histories often serve to increase the reader's understanding of the contribution it makes to the whole fabric of the medium. Our readers should be reminded, however, that they are likely to encounter "genre" titles in other sections of this guide because treatment emphases may have dictated more appropriate placements.

William Stedman follows a single genre through many media in his work *The Serials.* Tracing the serial's origin through comic strips and motion pictures of the early 1900s up to the present-day television soap operas, Stedman's history of the serial becomes a social and political chronicle of America. Equally nostalgic, although not quite as comprehensive, *The Great Television Series,* by Jeff Rovin, looks at the heroes of TV series beginning with Captain Video and Hopalong Cassidy and extending through such notables as Columbo and Wonder Woman. Even antihero Archie Bunker is included. Admittedly more popular than scholarly, this book is a pleasant blend of "fan-interest" information with valuable historical analysis of the programs and the powers behind them.

In Gary Grossman's *Saturday Morning TV,* children's television serials from 1947 to 1980 are analyzed and classified according to 15 different genres, such as westerns, space travel, and cartoons. This book is a well-illustrated comprehensive history and is enormously valuable for anyone interested in this area of research.

Some of the best works available on the histories of various genres of television can be found in the Arno Press collection "Dissertations in Broadcasting." Three works from the collection stand out as especially significant. *Television's Private Eye: An Examination of Twenty Years of Programming of a Particular Genre, 1949–1969,* by Robert Larka, investigates the origins of the private eye; the critics and scholars who write about the programs; and the major themes, motifs, and plot types commonly occurring in this genre. This well-researched book would be a valuable addition to a TV history collection and provides interesting reading as well. Robert Bailey's *An Examination of Prime Time Network Television Special Programs, 1948–1966* is a quantitative study. It provides an accurate record of special programs and describes the trends, patterns, and characteristics of their scheduling, sponsorship, ratings, and functions. Donald Kirkley's *A Descriptive Study of*

the Network Television Western during the Seasons 1955–56—1962–63
investigates the origins of the western hero and the settings, themes,
plots, and literature of the TV western.

An outstanding work on television documentaries is *The Image
Decade: Television Documentary, 1965–1975* by Charles Hammond.
Divided into four sections, Part I introduces the reader to the origin
and evolution of documentaries, defines the various documentary approaches, and reviews the growth of theme documentary in television.
Part II discusses the producer of documentaries and looks in depth at
individual producers who have made significant impact upon the role
of the documentary in American television. Part III explores the role
of the reporter in the documentary, and Part IV looks at individual documentary events. Hammond explores the role that a number of documentaries had in shaping American public opinion and policy and analyzes the techniques used to communicate effectively the various
themes. The innumerable detailed examples used by Hammond are invaluable in presenting a clear picture of the role the documentary
played during the turbulent sixties and seventies. The source notes for
each chapter, the bibliography, and the index are all quite excellent.
A. William Bluem's *Documentary in American Television* traces the
roots of the documentary as it developed in America. Bluem looks at
the social and technical implications of such developments as photography, broadcasting, and film as well as the all-important role that television played in making this form of communication viable. This work
is seminal and belongs in all media collections.

On the lighter side of television genres are two books—one dealing
with what was widely regarded as television vaudeville and the other
with TV game shows. *A Thousand Sundays: The Story of the Ed Sullivan Show,* by Jerry Bowles, chronicles 23 years of Sullivan's "Toast of
the Town" television show and, in the process, reveals the foibles and
the little-known offstage, petty tyrannies of one of TV's most celebrated
showmen. Sandwiched between the jugglers, the dancing bears, and
other cornball acts were the high culture artists such as Margot Fon-
teyn, Maria Callas, Eugene List, and the Russian Moiseyev Ballet. To
please middle America, Sullivan brought on Presley, the Beatles, Bogart, and Hope. An astute "reader" of the American pulse, Sullivan's
reign was unparalleled—he was king of the most powerful medium in
the world. While *TV Game Shows,* by Maxene Fabe, is written and mar-
keted as a pop culture, fan-oriented work, in reality it presents a solid
historical narrative of a generally overlooked programming form. A
40-page appendix gives an annotated chronological listing of game

shows from 1924 to 1979. The omission of an index is unfortunate, but overall this is a useful work.

BIBLIOGRAPHY

Bailey, Robert Lee. *An Examination of Prime Time Network Television Special Programs, 1948–1966.* New York: Arno, 1979.

Barnouw, Erik. *A History of Broadcasting in the United States.* Vol. 1 *A Tower in Babel;* Vol. 2 *The Golden Web;* Vol. 3 *The Image Empire.* New York: Oxford, 1966, 1968, 1970.

————. *Tube of Plenty: The Evolution of American Television.* New York: Oxford, 1975.

Bergreen, Laurence. *Look Now, Pay Later: The Rise of Network Broadcasting.* New York: Doubleday, 1980.

Bluem, William A. *Documentary in American Television: Form, Function and Method.* New York: Hastings House, 1965.

Bowles, Jerry. *A Thousand Sundays: The Story of the Ed Sullivan Show.* New York: Putnam, 1980.

Castleman, Harry, and Podrazik, Walter. *Watching TV: Four Decades of American Television.* New York: McGraw-Hill, 1982.

Czitrom, Daniel J. *Media and the American Mind: From Morse to McLuhan.* Chapel Hill, NC: University of North Carolina Press, 1982.

Fabe, Maxene. *TV Games Shows.* New York: Doubleday, 1979.

Fireman, Judy, ed. *TV Book: The Ultimate Television Book.* New York: Workman, 1977.

Gibson, George H. *Public Broadcasting: The Role of the Federal Government, 1912–76.* New York: Praeger, 1977.

Gordon, George N. *The Communications Revolution: A History of Mass Media in the United States.* New York: Hastings House, 1977.

Greenfield, Jeff. *Television: The First Fifty Years.* New York: Abrams, 1977.

Grossman, Gary. *Saturday Morning TV.* New York: Dell, 1981.

Hammond, Charles Montgomery. *The Image Decade: Television Documentary, 1965–1975.* New York: Hastings House, 1981.

Harris, Jay S., ed. and comp. *TV Guide: The First 25 Years.* New York: Simon & Schuster, 1978.

Head, Sydney, and Sterling, Christopher. *Broadcasting in America: A Survey of Television and Radio.* 4th ed. Boston: Houghton Mifflin, 1982.

Hess, Gary Newton. *An Historical Study of the DuMont Television Network.* New York: Arno, 1979.

Kirkley, Donald H. *A Descriptive Study of the Network Television Western during the Seasons 1955–56—1962–63.* New York: Arno, 1979.

Larka, Robert. *Television's Private Eye: An Examination of Twenty Years of Programming of a Particular Genre, 1949–1969.* New York: Arno, 1979.

Lichty, Lawrence Wilson, and Topping, Malachi C. *American Broadcasting: A Source Book on the History of Radio and Television.* New York: Hastings House, 1975.

O'Connor, John E., ed. *American History, American Television: Interpreting the Video Past.* New York: Frederick Ungar, 1983.

Rovin, Jeff. *The Great Television Series.* New York: A. S. Barnes, 1977.

Stamps, Charles Henry. *The Concept of the Mass Audience in American Broadcasting: An Historical Descriptive Study.* New York: Arno, 1979.

Stedman, Raymond William. *The Serials: Suspense and Drama by Installment.* 2d ed. Norman, OK: University of Oklahoma Press, 1977.

Sterling, Christopher H., and Kittross, John M. *Stay Tuned: A Concise History of American Broadcasting.* Belmont, CA: Wadsworth, 1978.

Stevens, John D., and Garcia, Hazel Dicken. *Communication History.* Beverly Hills, CA: Sage, 1980.

Udelson, Joseph H. *The Great Television Race: A History of the American Television Industry, 1925–1941.* University, AL: University of Alabama Press, 1982.

Wilk, Max. *The Golden Age of Television: Notes from the Survivors.* New York: Delacorte, 1976.

Chapter 3
Reference Sources

OVERVIEW

In this section, we are not discussing standard indexes that include coverage of the literature of mass communication. Excluded, therefore, since they are expected to be part of a library's basic reference collection, are such tools as *Business Periodicals Index, The New York Times Index, Psychological Abstracts, Public Affairs Information Service (PAIS) The Readers' Guide to Periodical Literature, Resources in Education, Social Sciences Citation Index, Social Sciences Index,* and *Sociological Abstracts,* although all will include citations to the literature about television and other mass media. We are interested in the more specialized reference materials meeting the twin criteria of being affordable and useful. Such materials can be divided into three categories: (1) General and Specialized Bibliographies, (2) Source Books, and (3) Guides to Radio and Television Programs.

GENERAL AND SPECIALIZED BIBLIOGRAPHIES

Few bibliographic works are as highly regarded as Eleanor Blum's *Basic Books in the Mass Media.* Greatly expanding upon the first edition, Blum, whose MLS degree and doctorate in communications have eminently qualified her to produce such a considerable work, was guided by three basic objectives: (1) compile a reference tool for the field; (2) offer the student and researcher a varied menu of research resources; and (3) provide the librarian with a selection tool. The subtitle, "An Annotated, Selected Booklist Covering General Communication, Book Publishing, Broadcasting, Editorial Journalism, Film, Magazines, and Advertising," accurately describes the content. Two other general bibliographies that should be mentioned are *Mass Communication Effects and Processes,* by Thomas Gordon and Mary Ellen Verna, and *A Bibliography of Theses and Dissertations in Broadcasting, 1920–1973,* by John Kittross. The Gordon and Verna work brings together 25 years' worth of mass communication effects literature scattered throughout various reference sources and academic journals from 1950 to 1975. The Kittross publication tracks down dissertations and theses representing over 4,300 major studies about broadcasting from 1920 to 1973, the intent being to make available a "living tool" to what is perhaps the most painstaking research in the field.

An exciting bibliographic addition to the field is Joyce Post's *TV Guide 25 Year Index,* providing access to more than 14,000 articles published from 1953 to 1977. The *Index* contains 42,000 entries (35,000 subject and 7,000 author entries), with 4,000 cross-references. For years *TV Guide,* the largest-selling magazine in the world, was ignored by scholars and critics and considered not worth preserving. Either libraries did not subscribe to it at all, or if they did, all but the current issues were discarded. Thus, one of the most valuable resources chronicling television programming content was experiencing the same fate as the videotape records of that content—virtual extinction. Although only two complete sets of *TV Guide's* published editions exist (one at the Library of Congress and the other at *TV Guide's* Randor, Pennsylvania headquarters), libraries are now being offered the complete run of *TV Guide* in microfilm. The index, which is in hard copy, was compiled to provide access to this wealth of material.

Moving on to more sophisticated bibliographic works, we find a rich diversity of materials dealing with television and human behavior, television and children, and legal aspects of broadcasting.

The Rand Reports were prepared under a grant from the Edna McConnell Clark Foundation and compiled by George Comstock, assisted by teams of researchers and scholars. They concentrated primarily on the relevant scientific literature about television and human behavior. The three reports, each carrying the master title *Television and Human Behavior,* are best discussed separately. The first, subtitled "A Guide to the Pertinent Scientific Literature," is the result of a year-long literature search using 1960 as the beginning date and projecting beyond the published materials contained in it to "research in progress." This volume contains 2,300 items assembled into a "master bibliography," which is distinguished by keyword descriptions according to topic and, if applicable, methodology. The master bibliography is followed by 11 specialized bibliographies for the user's convenience. Therefore, the user is advised to begin with the narrower, more specific bibliographies and work from them to the master bibliography for fuller descriptive material.

The second volume, subtitled "The Key Studies," summarizes 450 studies, which have been divided into two parts: (1) Empirical Research, which covers such aspects as principal findings, design and methodology, and theory and discussion and (2) Theory, Review, and Nonempirical Works, which presents principal conclusions and theory and discussion. The summaries, refined by an evaluation of the data rather than by a mere restatement, have also been rated by a panel of qualified scientific researchers acting as judges of the interest and timeliness of the material. The third volume, subtitled "The Research Horizon, Future and Present," describes current research in the context of the influential community perspectives that may affect future research.

In considering the interrelationship of television and young people, three reference publications stand out. *Effects and Functions of Television: Children and Adolescents,* by Manfred Meyer and Ursula Nissen, covers the period 1970 to 1978. This bibliography deals with relevant materials in English, French, and German, but all foreign citations in the bibliography are also given in English. The bibliography is subdivided into 12 subject categories (e.g., Socialization, TV Violence, Prosocial Content), and these in turn are subdivided into two categories for age: children up to 12–13 years and adolescents. *Television's Impact on Children and Adolescents,* by Sara Lake, is divided into five major chapters that cover the TV viewing habits of children; factors influencing their perception of TV and its impact; TV as a teaching tool; and the positive steps that might be taken to improve TV's possible impact. The materials cited are categorized according to document format, and additional information is given to facilitate user access. John P. Murray's bibliography *Television and Youth* covers 25 years of research and commentary on the subject, including approximately 3,000 citations, 60 percent of which were published between 1975 and 1980. The research is also multidiscipline and multinational and is cited as a timely aid to researchers, broadcasters, legislators, and others involved in the serious task of evaluating TV's impact on young people.

Taking a somewhat different approach, the *Yearbook of Broadcasting Articles* has been proclaimed as "the beginning of something new." This first volume, an "Anthology Edition" covering the period 1959–1978, lays the foundation for subsequent yearbooks. Its objective is to publish seminal essays from prominent legal periodicals and to discuss the most salient policy issues in the broadcasting industry. To avoid any error, the articles appearing in Volume I have been photographically reproduced. They are arranged in chronological order. An asset to this anthology is its four indexes: author, leading case, FCC reports and orders, and subject.

Everett Rogers, Linda Williams, and Rhonda B. West compiled the *Bibliography of the Diffusion of Innovations,* a holdings list of the 2,750 publications in the Diffusion Documents Center at Stanford University. The *Bibliography* includes two types of publications: (1) empirical diffusion studies (coded as "E:) and (2) nonempirical diffusion publications (coded as "N:), which in turn includes additional bibliographies, theoretical writings, and summarized findings of other diffusion publications.

SOURCE BOOKS

Although the descriptors "weighty," "dry," and "uninteresting" may apply to source books in general, media source books—ponderous with facts and figures though they may be—reflect dynamic and changing times. Consider, for example, *Les Brown's Encyclopedia of Television,* (1982), which was first published in 1977 under the title *The New York Times Encyclopedia of Television.* Les Brown refers to the years between editions as "the most turbulent years in the history of broadcasting" and names this interval Television II. Television II is the age of the new television technology, network reorganization and change, the seesaw pattern of public television, the deregulation of commercial and cable TV, and the reform movement of the Religious New Right. Brown includes nearly 400 new articles and hundreds of updated, rewritten entries in the new edition. He also gives us a full panoramic view of the TV industry, both behind and in front of the small screen. Readers find themselves reliving many of television's golden moments, learning new facts, or recalling forgotten ones. The author's penetrating analysis of the economic and political forces that have shaped this medium showcases his considerable talents as a historian.

The next two books to be considered, the 1977–1979 edition of William Rivers's *Aspen Handbook on the Media* and Craig and Peter Norback's *TV Guide Almanac,* are important for the diversity of information they contain. The *Aspen Handbook* is divided into 13 sections, which cover such topics as academic and nonacademic institutional communications research programs, communication organizations, media action groups, and print and nonprint media.

The *TV Guide Almanac,* compiled and edited by Craig and Peter Norback and the editors of *TV Guide* magazine, contains an eclectic array of information about a wide variety of topics ranging from the top 100 TV advertisers to audience research organizations; college TV stations; histories of TV and the networks; and various TV agencies, organizations, and associations. The index is lengthy and a necessary key to the content.

The *International Television Almanac,* edited by Richard Gortner, began publication in 1929 and continues to be an invaluable source of information on the TV industry. It features a lengthy "Who's Who" section of industry professionals, industry statistics, TV producers- distributors, equipment suppliers, advertising and publicity manufacturers, and much more. A new section, appearing for the first time in the 1984 edition, is a complete list of all made-for-TV movies of the 1982–1983 season, including appropriate credits for major artists and an expanded section on cable.

Inaugurated over a decade ago, *Educational Media Yearbook,* which began publication in 1973 and has recently released its ninth volume, has held to its initial goal: "Collecting in one volume significant information about educational media/instructional technology activities needed and used by professionals in the interrelated fields of educational/instructional technology, librarianship, communications (including telecommunications) and aspects of information science" (p.v). Editors James and Shirley Brown have divided their book into six parts: (1) Media in Training (an overview, not included in earlier volumes, covering media-related trends, opportunities, and problems); (2) Educational Technology: Status Reports (a review of the field); (3) Guide to Organizations and Associations; (4) Doctoral and Master's Programs; (5) Directory of Funding Sources; and (6) Mediagraphy (a reference tool for locating media about media). A comprehensive index is included.

For those researchers interested in studying television news in depth, George Washington University has published an extensive reference guide to news archives and information sources called *Television News Resources,* prepared by Fay Schreibman. Precise in detail, the guide provides information on collections, policies for use, and fee schedules, along with numerous finding aids.

Two books, *The Mass Media: Aspen Institute Guide to Communication Industry Trends,* by Christopher Sterling and Timothy Haight, and *Who Owns the Media?,* by Benjamin Compaine, are important because they bring together a great deal of statistical and factual data that are not easily found. In the Sterling and Haight book, the data are organized into more than 300 tables, which provide a sense of where the mass communication industry has been and where it is going. The book is organized into seven general subject categories including Ownership,

Economics, Content, and Audience, rather than according to specific medium, to facilitate what cross-comparisons among media the reader may wish to make. The Compaine volume, on the other hand, focuses on the questions of competition and concentration of ownership in the mass communications industry through the presentation of tabular data and the findings of other researchers regarding competition. Finally, a macro- and a microanalysis of the industry is attempted. The contribution that both books make goes a long way toward laying the groundwork for answering some very hard policy and regulatory questions.

Who's Who in Television and Cable, edited by Steven H. Scheuer, is the first in a new reference series covering leading personalities in the television, video, and cable industries. The editor acknowledges that because of the constraints of time and space, he was forced to limit his selection to 2,000 individuals, but that he selected network, public television and cable network executives, hundreds of on-the-air TV personalities of national repute, and local TV station executives located in the nation's television centers (New York, Washington, DC, and Los Angeles).

Another new reference book is *Longman Dictionary of Mass Media and Communication* (1982), by Tracy Daniel Connors, which defines 7,000 terms covering the fields of advertising, public relations, book and magazine publishing, journalism, photography, broadcasting, film, and theatre. On the other hand, a source book which is an old standby, *A Taxonomy of Concepts in Communication* (1975), by Reed Blake and Edwin Haroldsen, still serves as a useful guide to the vocabulary of communication. In this guide, each concept is cross-referenced with related concepts, challenging students to systematically expand their inventories and understanding of the key terms and concepts that characterize the field.

Finally, there are two specialized source books that deserve mention: Frank Kahn's *Documents of American Broadcasting* and *Women and the Mass Media,* by Matilda Butler and William Paisley. Kahn's book, now in its fourth edition, is unique in that it presents primary source materials in the field of broadcasting. Included are laws, speeches, codes, decisions, reports, and FCC materials—all in their original form. The new fourth edition (1984) completely updates the third (1978) by including the most recent changes in the Communications Act of 1934 and the broadcasting deregulatory documents of the FCC and the Supreme Court. In addition, the author includes a completely new section, "Understanding Law," designed to acquaint the neophyte with proper legal citation and legal terminology. There is also a dual table of contents (one in standard format and the second according to thematic pattern) as well as a dual index (one general, the other according to cited cases).

Presenting an overview on the status of women in the mass communications industry and their portrayal by the media, *Women and Mass Media* includes a little of everything—a bibliographic guide, how-to-do-it information, and an agenda for improvement and change. The basic idea the authors promote is that sexism exists in multifarious forms—in language, image, and content—and that to combat it requires an awareness of it.

GUIDES TO RADIO AND TELEVISION PROGRAMS

One of the greatest sources of frustration for the electronic media scholar who wishes to study a program document in its original form is locating program tapes. There is virtually no correlation between level and quality of print libraries and their audiovisual archival counterparts. For this reason, those books that attempt to reconstruct and capture the essence of the sounds and images of programs that have long since been committed only to the folklore of the mind are to be doubly valued. Guides to television programs have been appearing on the market with some regularity and thus may pose a problem for the reader who may not know which ones to buy. Yet, those who would buy one such guide would probably buy several; in a sense, it is analogous to buying several cookbooks because each might contain something different. Two books deal with the total TV program panorama: *Complete Encyclopedia of Television Programs, 1947–1979*, by Vincent Terrace, and *Total Television: A Comprehensive Guide to Programming from 1948 to 1980*, by Alex McNeil. Terrace boasts that "every known entertainment no matter how obscure, from 1947 to 1979, has been included" (p. [8]). Supplementing the core of the book—nearly 3,500 network and syndicated programs, including imports—are more than 200 photographs and a comprehensive index. The McNeil guide includes the following extras in addition to its primary listing of 3,400 series: a chronological list of 570 TV specials, the networks' prime time fall schedules from 1948 to 1979, the Emmy and Peabody Award winners since 1948, a list of the top-rated series for each year, and an index of names. *The Complete Directory to Prime Time Network TV Shows 1946–Present* by Tim Brooks and Earle Marsh, concentrates on prime time and includes a history of network television, a listing of the longest running series on prime time and series airing on more than one network, a listing of TV hit songs from individual telecasts as well as from series, and a name index.

Taking a different approach, *Television Drama Series Programming,* by Larry Gianakos, is a four-volume set, covering the periods 1947–1959, 1959–1975, 1975–1980, and 1980–1982. Gianakos lists series programs season by season, giving titles of episodes within the series, date of broadcast, and regular guest performers. His work, although narrower in scope, is a good supplement to the three program guides described above. It is indexed by series title.

Known in the trade as the "bible" for programs in syndication, *Series, Serials, & Packages,* published annually by the Broadcast Information Bureau, lists TV film series and taped shows in domestic and foreign-language editions. Entries include title, time, number of films or tapes, storyline, year produced, sponsor, TV distributor, and producer.

In the same vein as the retrospective guides are annual records of TV programs, the most consistent of which has been Nina David's *TV Season,* which began with the 1974–1975 season. It lists information for programs presented by the three commercial networks and PBS, including currently produced and nationally distributed syndicated programs. It also features several additional listings, such as "Shows by Program Type," "Shows Captioned or Translated for the Hearing Impaired," "Cancelled Shows," "New Shows," "New and Cancelled Shows," "Summer Shows," and both the Emmy Awards and Peabody Awards. There is also an index entitled "Who's Who in TV."

TV: The Television Annual, 1978–1979, conceived and edited by Steven H. Scheuer, is a colorful and lusty yearbook capturing the most significant aspects of American network television, but its continuity remains in question. It also features several perceptive essays, a bibliography, and an index of names of personalities and programs.

Finally, there are specialized records of programs or actors or directors that are beginning to appear. The CBS News compilation *60 Minutes Verbatim* contains the complete text of the 114 stories broadcast on that program during the 1979 season; James Parish's *Actors' Television Credits* covers the periods 1950–1951 in one volume and two supplements; and Christopher Wicking and Tise Vahimagi's *The American Vein: Directors and Directions in Television* covers films made for TV (1948–1978), classified according to the directors who made them.

Regarding the various types of reference books we have discussed, we should point out that our listing may not be all inclusive, but we believe it conveys the message that a semblance of respectability is beginning to take shape in resources and guides for the serious television researcher.

BIBLIOGRAPHY

Blake, Reed H., and Haroldsen, Edwin O. *A Taxonomy of Concepts in Communication.* New York: Hastings House, 1975.

Blum, Eleanor. *Basic Books in the Mass Media: An Annotated, Selected Book List Covering General Communications, Book Publishing, Broadcasting, Editorial Journalism, Film, Magazines, and Advertising.* 2d ed. Urbana, IL: University of Illinois Press, 1980.

Brooks, Tim, and Marsh, Earle. *The Complete Directory to Prime Time Network TV Shows, 1946–Present.* New York: Ballantine, 1979.

Brown, James W., and Brown, Shirley N., eds. *Educational Media Yearbook, 1984.* 10th ed. Littleton, CO: Libraries Unlimited, 1984.

Brown, Les. *Les Brown's Encyclopedia of Television.* New York: Zoetrope, 1982.

Butler, Matilda, and Paisley, William. *Women and the Mass Media: Sourcebook for Research and Action.* New York: Human Science Press, 1980.

CBS, Inc. CBS News. *60 Minutes Verbatim. Who Said What to Whom: The Complete Text of 114 Stories with Mike Wallace, Morley Safer, Dan Rather, Harry Reasoner, and Andy Rooney.* New York: Arno, 1980.

Compaine, Benjamin M. *Who Owns the Media? Concentration of Ownership in the Mass Communications Industry.* New York: Harmony Books, 1979.

Comstock, George A., et al. *Television and Human Behavior: The Key Studies.* Santa Monica, CA: Rand, 1975.

Comstock, George A., and Fisher, Marilyn. *Television and Human Behavior: A Guide to the Pertinent Scientific Literature.* Santa Monica, CA: Rand, 1975.

Comstock, George A., and Lindsey, Georg. *Television and Human Behavior: The Research Horizon, Future and Present.* Santa Monica, CA: Rand, 1975.

Connors, Tracy Daniel. *Longman Dictionary of Mass Media and Communication.* New York: Longman, 1982.

David, Nina, ed. and comp. *TV Season.* Phoenix, AZ: Oryx Press, 1976.

Gianakos, Larry James. *Television Drama Series Programming: A Comprehensive Chronicle, 1947–1959.* Metuchen, NJ: Scarecrow, 1980.

———. *Television Drama Series Programming: A Comprehensive Chronicle, 1959–1975.* Metuchen, NJ: Scarecrow, 1978.

———. *Television Drama Series Programming: A Comprehensive Chronicle, 1975–1980.* Metuchen, NJ: Scarecrow, 1981.

———. *Television Drama Series Programming: A Comprehensive Chronicle, 1980–1982.* Metuchen, NJ: Scarecrow, 1983.

Gordon, Thomas Frank, and Verna, Mary Ellen. *Mass Communication Effects and Processes: A Comprehensive Bibliography, 1950–1975.* Beverly Hills, CA: Sage, 1978.

Gortner, Richard, ed. *International Television Almanac, 1984.* 29th ed. New York: Quigley, 1984.

Kahn, Frank. *Documents of American Broadcasting.* 4th ed. Englewood Cliffs, NJ: Prentice-Hall, 1984.

Kittross, John M. *A Bibliography of Theses and Dissertations in Broadcasting. 1920–1973.* Washington, DC: Broadcast Education Association, 1978.

Lake, Sara. *Television's Impact on Children and Adolescents.* Phoenix, AZ: Oryx Press, 1981.

McNeil, Alex. *Total Television: A Comprehensive Guide to Programming from 1948–1980.* New York: Penguin, 1980.

Meyer, Manfred, and Nissen, Ursula. *Effects and Functions of Television. Children and Adolescents: A Bibliography of Selected Literature, 1970–1978.* Munchen, Germany: K.G. Saur, 1981; Hamden, CT: Linnet Books, 1981.

Murray, John P. *Television and Youth: 25 Years of Research and Controversy.* Boys Town, NE: The Boys Town Center for the Study of Youth Development, 1980.

Norback, Craig T., and Norback, Peter G. *TV Guide Almanac.* New York: Ballantine, 1980.

Parish, James Robert. *Actors' Television Credits, 1950–1972.* Metuchen, NJ: Scarecrow, 1973.

Parish, James Robert, and Terrace, Vincent. *Actors' Television Credits: Supplement 2.* Metuchen, NJ: Scarecrow, 1982.

Parish, James Robert, with Trost, Mark. *Actors' Television Credits: Supplement 1.* Metuchen, NJ: Scarecrow, 1978.

Post, Joyce A. *TV Guide 25 Year Index, April 3, 1953–Dec. 31, 1977: By Author and Subject.* Edited by Catherine E. Johnson. Randor, PA: Triangle Publications, 1979.

Rivers, William L.; Thompson, Wallace; and Nyhan, Michael J. *Aspen Handbook on the Media: A Selective Guide to Research, Organizations and Publications in Communications, 1977–79.* New York: Praeger, 1977.

Rogers, Everett M.; Williams, Linda; and West, Rhonda B. *Bibliography of the Diffusion of Innovations.* Stanford, CA: Institute for Communication Research, 1977.

Scheuer, Steven H. *Who's Who in Television and Cable.* New York: Facts on File, 1983.

Scheuer, Steven H., ed. *TV: The Television Annual, 1978–79: A Complete Record of American Television from June 1, 1978 through May 31, 1979.* New York: Macmillan, 1979.

Schreibman, Fay C. *Television News Resources: A Guide to Collections.* Washington, DC: Television News Study Center, Resources and Media Resources Dept., Gelman Library, George Washington University, 1981.

Series, Serials, & Packages. Domestic ed. Syosset, NY: Broadcast Information Bureau, 1974–.

Series, Serials, & Packages. Foreign Language ed. Syosset, NY: Broadcast Information Bureau, 1974–.

Sterling, Christopher H., and Haight, Timothy R. *The Mass Media: Aspen Institute Guide to Communication Industry Trends.* New York: Praeger, 1978.

Terrace, Vincent. *The Complete Encyclopedia of Television Programs, 1947–1979.* 2d ed. rev. San Diego, CA: A.S. Barnes, 1979.

Wicking, Christopher, and Vahimagi, Tise. *The American Vein: Directors and Directions in Television.* New York: Dutton, 1979.

Yearbook of Broadcasting Articles. 1959–78. Washington, DC: Federal Publications, Inc., 1980.

Part II
The Environment

Introduction

No other aspect of the mass communication process has been as assiduously studied and researched or has inspired as much commentary and controversy as that of media influence on the environment, including the media's impact on news and politics. In this section, we begin with benchmark studies that lay the foundation for understanding this area of scholarship and research while also serving as useful historical demarcations for the prevailing ideas of the time.

Interestingly, in the brief history of the discipline, the question of media influence has taken on a chameleon-like characteristic, with scholars and researchers differing dramatically on the precise nature of the media's influences, both in the quantitative and qualitative dimensions. After several seemingly contradictory stances, the discipline seems to have come full circle in its thinking, but careful study reveals that there are differences in the subtleties and shadings of today's research on effects.

The earliest studies in this area concentrate heavily on the historical, legal, and content aspects of print and the electronic media of the time. During the period between the two world wars, the field was infused by the thinking of scholars and researchers from other disciplines, notably social psychology and political science. Armed with their own particular theoretical perspectives, research skills, and methodologies, they attempted to assess the impact of the mass media in areas specifically related to their own disciplines. In the process, they generated a great deal of excitement because their studies suggested the media to be all powerful. For example, the media were likened to hypodermic needles injecting a passive audience with mysterious potions that controlled their minds and thoughts or to magic bullets that unerringly hit their targets and figuratively caused their audiences to fall over, dead. It was the period of mechanistic stimulus-response belief, promulgated by the analyses of the powerful influences of wartime propaganda, which virtually made mush of people's minds. Such studies as *The Symbolic Instrument in Early Times,* the first volume of the series "Propaganda and Communication in World History," edited by Harold

Lasswell, et al., and George Bruntz's *Allied Propaganda and the Collapse of the German Empire in 1918* are representative of these views. However, additional support for the powerful effects concept was to come from other quarters: in the studies of radio's content and audience, *Radio Research, 1941* and *Radio Research, 1942–1943,* by Paul Lazarsfeld and Frank Stanton; in the classic study by Robert Merton of Kate Smith's phenomenal war bond drive, *Mass Persuasion;* and in the study of the astounding fallout of fear and panic caused by Orson Welles's infamous radio broadcast of H.G. Wells's *War of the Worlds* as analyzed in Hadley Cantril's *The Invasion from Mars.* Although the concept of the bullet or hypodermic needle penetrating a helpless audience has generally been discarded by serious researchers, there are those members of the public today who still believe that the media hold superordinate powers over the minds of people.

The next period, encompassing the years between 1940 and 1960, saw a shift in thinking from the powerful influences model to a limited effects model. One of the principal proponents of this view was Carl Hovland who, with his colleagues at Yale, carried out a number of experimental studies growing out of the Army's need to develop strategies to improve morale after an assessment of the attitudes and opinions of servicemen and civilians toward World War II. *Experiments on Mass Communication* and *Communication and Persuasion* are examples of their work. The classic studies of the effects of mass communication on political campaigns, carried out by Paul Lazarsfeld, Bernard Berelson, and their associates and published as *The People's Choice* and *Voting,* demonstrated that family and peers exert a greater influence on voting decisions than the media. A few years later, Elihu Katz and Paul Lazarsfeld published their seminal study, *Personal Influence,* n which they introduced their theory of the two-step flow concept of opinion leaders who receive information from the media and pass it on to their peers along with their own interpretations. Once again, the notion of mediating influences reducing the power of the mass media comes into play. Finally, we must cite the landmark volume by Joseph Klapper, *The Effects of Mass Communication,* a masterful synthesis of research supporting the view that "mass communication [is] a contributory agent, but not the sole cause, in a process of reinforcing the existing conditions..." (p. 8); that certain mediating variables such as selective perception, selective exposure and selective retention, group relationships, and interpersonal influence are more important agents in affecting attitude, opinion, and behavior.

In the 1960s and 1970s, the limited effects model was refuted as being too narrow in scope and new assumptions were formulated supporting a moderate effects view of mass communication. Primary among these were (1) the limited effects model understated the dimension and salience of mass communication effects; (2) such variables as attitudes and opinions were not the most appropriate ones to focus upon; (3) the research of the past looking at mass communication as doing something to the audience member was too one-sided and may well be turned around to look at what the audience member does with mass communication; and (4) past research, in concentrating on short-term effects, may have almost totally excluded from consideration the question of long-term effects. Research within this period concentrated on the uses and gratifications, agenda-setting, and cultural norms approaches. Jay Blumler and Denis McQuail's study, *Television in Politics: Its Uses and Influence,* was important for yielding insights on the relationship between the audience member's needs and motives and knowledge about effects. In essence, such research supports the concept of the obstinate, active audience rather than the passive audience of earlier research. *The Emergence of American Political Issues* by Donald Shaw and Maxwell McCombs, explores the agenda-setting function of the press in which a strong positive relationship was established between what people determined as the most salient campaign issues and what the media established as important. Melvin DeFleur's cultural norms theory postulated that the media influence social norms through their presentations of what constitutes appropriate behavior. This appeared to be a promising theory; yet, the third and fourth editions of DeFleur's *Theories of Mass Communication* dropped this concept, which had appeared in the two earlier editions.

In the late 1960s, a revival of interest in the concept of the powerful media effects model began to emerge on the research horizon. This time, however, rather than confining attention to attitude or behavioral change, a broader view was taken, as researchers pondered and studied a whole range of related and important influences, such as the audience's self-concept and role expectations, their leisure time pursuits, their perceptions of the world, their codes of ethics and views of moral and immoral behavior, their knowledge of public issues, their satisfaction levels, and other impinging aspects of the human experience. It must be pointed out, however, that the media cannot be studied in isolation without taking into account the prevailing sociopolitical climate of the times. Thus, the media's influences are consonant with the ups and downs of economic and social barometers. In times of war and economic instability, people are more receptive to persuasive communications, and the media exert greater power. During periods of peace and prosperity, people are less likely to be looking for answers. Because they are satisfied with their lives, they prefer the status quo and become resistant to change. Hence, the media's effects are likely to be limited. Methodological considerations in mass communication research must also be taken into account. The controlled research of the laboratory in which subjects are exposed to communication situations under optimum conditions is likely to produce more dramatic results. Field research, on the other hand, in which the variables of real life are likely to become complicated and confounded by uncontrolled influences, has predictably produced lesser effects—but this, too, is changing because of the more advanced research measurement and analysis techniques available today. With this introductory overview, we will now turn our attention to specific subject areas of media effects.

BIBLIOGRAPHY

Berelson, Bernard R.; Lazarsfeld, Paul F.; and McPhee, William N. *Voting: A Study of Opinion Formation in a Presidential Campaign.* Chicago: University of Chicago Press, 1966.

Blumler, Jay G., and McQuail, Denis. *Television in Politics: Its Uses and Influence.* Chicago: University of Chicago Press, 1969.

Bruntz, George. *Allied Propaganda and the Collapse of the German Empire in 1918.* Palo Alto, CA: Stanford University Press, 1938.

Cantril, Hadley; Gaudet, Hazel; and Herzog, Herta. *The Invasion from Mars: A Study in the Psychology of Panic.* Princeton, NJ: Princeton University Press, 1940.

DeFleur, Melvin L., and Ball-Rokeach, Sandra. *Theories of Mass Communication. 4th ed.* New York: Longman, 1982.

Hovland, Carl Iver; Janis, Irving L.; and Kelley, Harold H. *Communication and Persuasion.* New Haven, CT: Yale University Press, 1953.

Hovland, Carl Iver; Lumsdaine, Arthur A.; and Sheffield, Fred D. *Experiments on Mass Communication.* Princeton, NJ: Princeton University Press, 1949.

Katz, Elihu, and Lazarsfeld, Paul F. *Personal Influence: The Part Played by People in the Flow of Communications.* Glencoe, IL: Free Press, 1955.

Klapper, Joseph T. *The Effects of Mass Communication.* Glencoe, IL: Free Press, 1960.

Lasswell, Harold D.; Learner, Daniel; and Speier, Hans, eds. *The Symbolic Instrument in Early Times.* Honolulu, HI: East-West Center, University of Hawaii, 1979.

Lazarsfeld, Paul Felix, and Stanton, Frank N. *Radio Research, 1941.* New York: Duell, Sloan and Pearce, 1941.

———. *Radio Research, 1942–1943.* New York: Duell, Sloan and Pearce, 1944.

Lazarsfeld, Paul Felix; Berelson, Bernard; and Gaudet, Hazel. *The People's Choice: How the Voter Makes up His Mind in a Presidential Campaign.* 3d ed. New York: Columbia University Press, 1968.

Merton, Robert King. *Mass Persuasion: The Social Psychology of a War Bond Drive.* New York: Harper, 1946.

Shaw, Donald Lewis, and McCombs, Maxwell E. *The Emergence of American Political Issues: The Agenda-Setting Function of the Press.* St. Paul, MN: West, 1977.

Chapter 4
Television Processes and
Effects: The Big Picture

OVERVIEW

In this chapter, the broader aspects of the television processes and effects are surveyed before going on to Chapter 5, which deals more specifically with television and children. The more than 50 titles included here are divided among four areas: General Perspectives, Theory and Research, Audience, and Content. In the first section, we lay a solid groundwork for a complex, multifaceted, and sometimes seemingly shifting field. Thus we rely on many older works that have become classics in the field (i.e., the works of Schramm and Roberts, Klapper, Comstock) but juxtapose them against some of the newer perspectives of Baran, Primeau, Esslin, and Berman. The section "Theory and Research" includes those works that bring into focus the major research milestones that highlight the last 60 years of mass communication study and research. In the section "Television Audience" we look at the audience from the varied perspectives of aggregate, mass, social group, and market. The final section, "Content," grapples with problems of categorization, but we feel the result is a fair and representative sampling of those works that, taken together, contribute to an appreciation of the richness and depth of the message.

GENERAL PERSPECTIVES

Before turning our attention to specific subject areas of television's effects, we believe it fundamental to deal with the more general aspects of the TV environment. Here, the works of Wilbur Schramm and George Comstock, in addition to the previously cited landmark volume by Joseph Klapper, stand out. In the second edition of Schramm and

Robert's *The Process and Effects of Mass Communication*, the point is made that during the period between the first edition (1954) and the second (1971), a greater number of books on the subject of communication research was published than in the entire history of that discipline up to 1954. The 1971 edition is divided into two main sections which study (1) the nature of communication between humans (covering media, messages, and audiences of mass communication) and (2) the nature of communication effects (covering attitude information/effects, social effects, public opinion and politics, innovation and change, and the technological future of mass communication).

The ambitious undertaking by George Comstock and his associates resulted in a comprehensive volume entitled *Television and Human Behavior*. Published in 1978, Comstock's book synthesizes the information contained in more than 2,500 books, articles, reports, and other documents and is a fine example of the retrieval and synthesis of scientific information. The book covers types of television programs, themes, and messages; the size, characteristics, and viewing habits of the viewing audience, including their attitudes toward the medium; and four specific segments of the audience: women, Blacks, the poor, and the elderly. Data are also presented on television and politics and on television and advertising, each area providing important insights in terms of similarities and differences in their attempts to persuade. Finally, the area of the psychology of behavioral effects is considered in relation to perceptions of program content (for example, the state of physiological arousal and perceived reality or authenticity of the television portrayal). An agenda for future research concludes this overview.

There are several books that provide a broad overview of media systems and effects, combining fundamental theoretical perspectives with current controversy and problems prevalent in the media. Among such books are W. Phillips Davison, et al., *Mass Media: Systems and Effects;* Charlene Brown, Trevor Brown, and William Rivers, *The Media and the People;* Don Pember, *Mass Media in America;* and George Comstock, *Television in America.* The Davison book is outstanding, especially for its material on contrasting media systems; Brown for his strong historical approach; and Pember for his unflinching emphasis on the increasing commercialization of the media. Comstock's *Television in America* is a broad introductory analysis of the social consequences of television. Although primarily a condensed version of previously published works by Comstock, it still stands out as a unique and useful contribution to the literature of television.

Two books that are designed to heighten self-awareness as to how the mass media might be used in dealing with society's problems and questions are *Using the Mass Media,* by Steven Chaffee and Michael J. Petrich, and *Mass Communication and Everyday Life,* by Dennis K. Davis and Stanley J. Baran. The problems that Chaffee and Petrich discuss include those dealing with public information concerning the courts, schools, military, and business; influencing consumers and voters; and the media as agencies of social control in areas of violence, ecology, sex, and political radicalism. Davis and Baran present several approaches to aid in the understanding of mass communication, including their own frame analysis concept. According to the authors, "framing" is making sense of a situation through the application of codes to guide perceptions of behavior in specific situations.

Unique in terms of its emphasis and direction, *Television and Social Behavior: Beyond Violence and Children,* edited by Stephen B. Withey and Ronald P. Abeles, is the report of the Social Science Research Council (SSRC) committee on Television and Social Behavior. The premise was that the SSRC committee would not only assess the various measures of violence but would also suggest new directions for research that would go beyond the emphasis on children and violence. The committee's early decisions included an examination of TV's influence on adults, especially the elderly and minority groups; an assessment of the violence profile; and a building on, rather than a duplication of, the work of other groups such as the Rand Corporation and the Reston Conference.

Three titles deal with the "language" of television, although on different levels. Ronald Primeau applies the principles of rhetoric to analyze television programs in his book, *The Rhetoric of Television.* He defines these principles as invention, arrangement, style, delivery, and memory. In explaining each of these concepts within the context of such program genres as news, soap operas, situation comedies, game shows, and advertising, Primeau supplies the reader with numerous examples and provides various charts and exercises, as well as questions, for the reader to test his or her own mettle. Michael Geis, in *The Language of Television Advertising,* applies the perspectives of psycholinguistics to illustrate how words, phrases, and intonations are used by advertisers and how consumers, in turn, interpret them. The authors address advertising intended for both adults and children. The third title, *The Age of Television,* by Martin Esslin, takes broader aim and defines the language of television as being "drama," hence entertainment. Thus, Esslin reasons, the viewer has come to expect reality programming—news, documentaries, political broadcasts—to contain the same elements of entertainment as he or she would expect from fictional content.

Two books dealing with the diffusion of information are *Public Communication Campaigns,* edited by Ronald Rice and William Paisley, and *Advertising and Social Change,* by Ronald Berman. *Public Communication Campaigns* is a rich blend of historical and theoretical perspectives, case studies, and prescriptive approaches to this long-overlooked area. Taken as a whole, the 14 articles in this work offer the reader an invaluable handbook on the theory and strategy for creating and evaluating effective public information campaigns. This book fills a critical void in the literature while at the same time meeting a practical need in the field. The Ronald Berman title ventures beyond the traditional view of advertising as a means to persuade consumers to buy products. According to the author, the role of advertising is to reflect our conceptions of actual and normative social behavior. Berman, therefore, presents advertising as a new kind of American institution and suggests that it is in need of critical evaluation and understanding.

THEORY AND RESEARCH

Four volumes from the series "Sage Annual Reviews of Communication Research" are invaluable resources on mass communication research and its future. Each volume provides a forum for the expanded discussion of important issues and suggests new approaches in the study of social communication. The 1977 volume, *Strategies for Communication Research,* edited by Paul Hirsch, Peter Miller, and F. Gerald Kline, discusses mass media organizations, measurement strategies, and the concept of time. *Current Perspectives in Mass Communication Research,* edited by Gerald Kline and Philip Tichenor, presents a wide-ranging overview of the nature and extent of mass communication research. Jay Blumler and Elihu Katz have assembled a fascinating group of studies that take as their primary focus the state of gratifications research in *The Uses of Mass Communication. New Models for Mass Communication Research,* edited by Peter Clarke, looks at human information processing within the context of new research models. A fifth work, edited by Daniel Lerner and Lyle Nelson, *Communication Research: A Half-Century Appraisal,* is an appropriate tribute to Wilbur Schramm (to whom the book is dedicated) through its coverage of Schramm's major areas of research interests—the role of communication in education and development, the analysis of communication issues, and policy implications in communication. Together, these five works present a comprehensive integration of mass communication research by incorporating multiple approaches to research design and implementation, theoretical orientations, and analytical perspectives in a highly readable collection of empirical studies, critical essays, and reviews of the research literature.

Another group of books serve as an important road map to mass communication theory and research in that by reviewing the past, they illuminate the future. The first, *Milestones in Mass Communication Research: Media Effects,* by Shearon Lowery and Melvin DeFleur, covers the most ground by presenting 11 watershed studies conducted over the past 60 years. They cover virtually all of the media from film (The Payne Fund Studies) to comic books (Seduction of the Innocent: The Great Comic Books Scare). In keeping with DeFleur's earlier writings, the interactive nature of mass communication and society is emphasized by the authors, and an overall evolutionary perspective is presented.

The next major step is represented by the two-volume Government Printing Office publication, *Television and Behavior: Ten Years of Scientific Progress and Implication for the Eighties,* which tracks the research of the past decade. A "Summary Report" (Volume I) and "Technical Reviews" (Volume II), while offering an update of the 1972 Surgeon General's report of television's impact on children, is to be valued as an expansion into other topical areas of concern. The Cognitive and Affective Aspects of Television, Violence and Aggression; Social Beliefs and Social Behavior; Television and Social Relations; Television and Health; and Television in American Society are the major categories into which the more than two dozen reports have been divided.

The third publication is Dennis Howitt's *The Mass Media and Social Problems.* The overall plan of this book is to divide the content between theoretical perspectives and a review of research that has been carried out on such social problems as violence, sexism, pornography, education, health, crime, and courts as related to the mass media.

The role of the media in instructional media research is the subject of the following three titles. By far the most sophisticated of the three, *Interaction of Media, Cognition and Learning,* by Gavriel Salomon, relates the symbols of the medium to specific learning tasks. For example, the author relates those aspects of film and television that function as signs—"zooms," "cuts," "close-ups:—to the cognitive skills of the learner, thus laying the foundation for an exciting area of new research. The next two titles, *Using Mass Media for Learning,* edited by Roger Yarrington, and *Adult Learning and Public Broadcasting,* edited by Marilyn Kressel, approach television and postsecondary education from a more pragmatic perspective and should serve well as sources for faculty and administrators involved in teleducation.

In a class by itself, *Miscomprehension of Televised Communications,* by Jacob Jacoby, Wayne Hoyer, and David Sheluga, sets out to measure the rate of accuracy of the viewers' comprehension of television's advertising messages based on charges received by regulatory agencies that certain advertisers were deliberately misleading the public. The study measured the comprehension of nonadvertising messages as well, finding that the rate of miscomprehension of fictional program excerpts, compared to advertising messages, reached significance at the .01 level. The material covered in this study show the crucial need for continued research along these same lines and also the need to tackle the questions that the study raises with regard to weaknesses in the design of comparing intact messages (advertising) with messages taken out of context (nonadvertising).

Two titles on the electronic church have been selected for their breadth of coverage on a subject that is as timely as it is thought-provoking. *Prime Time Preachers: The Rising Power of Televangelism,* by Jeffrey Hadden and Charles Swann, analyzes the attributes and comparative effectiveness of 17 prominent "televangelists," size and demographic characteristics of their audiences, the economic and political impact of their telechurches, and their relationship with the FCC, among other topics. *Religious Television: The Experience in America.* written by Peter Horsfield, a practicing minister with research credentials, traces the development and rise of religious television, explores the research into the uses and effects of religious television, and speculates on the future of religious broadcasting.

To consider George Gordon's *Erotic Communications: Studies in Sex, Sin and Censorship* at this juncture may seem paradoxical, but Gordon's treatment of this subject, which is both analytical and objective, moves it to the level of scholarly discourse. Positing that erotic communication needs to be considered within the larger framework of human communication, Gordon divides his book into three sections: (1) a historical examination of the various media forms of erotic communications; (2) an up-to-date examination of the legal, moral, and functional perspectives of the field; and (3) an agenda of propositions for the future.

To conclude this section, we cite two volumes that explore the role of the media in effecting social change. The first, *Does Mass Communication Change Public Opinion after All? A New Approach to Effects Analysis,* by James Lemert, is a product of the author's disillusionment with the reductionist view. Its main strength lies in the questions the author raises with regard to the dimension of the linkages among the media, public opinion, and decision makers. The second volume, *Mass Media and Social Change,* edited by Elihu Katz, retraces the mold/mirror continuum with some provocative insights, not the least of which is that greater consideration be given to inter- and multidisciplinary approaches.

TELEVISION AUDIENCES

Described as "a sort of Kinsey Report on the medium with just about every TV statistic ever compiled," Leo Bogart's *The Age of Television* (first issued in 1956; updated in 1958 and 1972 with a set of notes to be read with the text) serves as an excellent overview of the medium and its audience. The author's intent is to show television's impact upon American life, particularly in relation to consumption patterns of other media and its effects upon spectator sports, advertising, politics, and young people.

More often than not, television is looked upon as "doing things" to us. The concept that the television viewer passively sits back and unquestioningly absorbs the output of the "tube" is widely held. Among the earliest and most comprehensive assessments of the television viewer, which debunks the concept of the passive viewer, is Gary Steiner's *The People Look at Television.* This seminal work, the result of a national survey conducted in 1960, examines television and its audience in three main areas: television as a medium, television as viewing, and television as content. The television-as-a-medium section sought information about television in comparison to other technical and social developments and services. The section on television as viewing queried the audience as to the satisfaction or frustration associated with the viewing process. The final section on television content focused on the viewers' responses to programming and advertising. A decade later, Robert Bower's *Television and the Public* updated Steiner's study, assessing the ensuing changes in public attitudes toward television. The most recent work in this area of television use is *The Public's Use of Television* (1980) by Ronald Frank and Marshall Greenberg. This book follows closely the efforts of Steiner and Bower, but with greater focus on television's relationship to other leisure activities, television's relationship to other media, and a segmentation scheme that describes how different types of audience members with varying interest patterns use television. These three works taken together offer an invaluable tracking of public attitudes toward and uses made of television over nearly a 20-year period.

Frank and Greenberg produced another study, *Audiences for Public Television* (1982), in which they expanded upon their earlier analysis while focusing on public television. As in their earlier work, audience interest segmentation categories are utilized, with the hope that programmers might utilize this information to improve their product.

One important area of audience research that is generally overlooked is specialized audiences. Three titles, however, stand out. The first, *Television and the Aging Audience,* by Richard Davis, explores the relationship that exists between older viewers and television as well as the ways in which television portrays the image of aging. Davis thoroughly covers the issues, controversies, and the content relating to the older person and television. A somewhat wider-ranging look at communications use by a specific group is *Use of the Mass Media by the Urban Poor,* by Bradley Greenberg and Brenda Dervin. This work, which represents the findings of three separate research projects, looks at the complete spectrum of communication behavior of the poor with a particular emphasis on mass communication. Part I looks at media use, availability, content preferences, and functions and attitudes toward the media. Part II is a review of the literature on communication behaviors of the poor, which summarizes about 80 studies and reports. The authors indicate that their intention is to provide a realistic picture of the poor's communication behaviors with the hope that future research and poverty programs will be built upon concrete information about those behaviors.

Finally, *Mexican Americans and the Mass Media,* by Bradley Greenberg, Michael Burgoon, Judee Burgoon, and Felipe Korzenny, reports on the research of project CASA (Communication and Spanish-Speaking Americans) and fills a critical gap in what is known about the mass communication behavior of the fastest growing U.S. minority. Divided into four sections, the book focuses on the mass and interpersonal communication patterns of Mexican Americans; the opinions of community and media executives with respect to the Mexican-American audience; and mass media preferences, uses, and attitudes of adults and younger audiences. Also presented is a summary of findings and implications.

TELEVISION CONTENT

When Marshall McLuhan articulated his now famous aphorism, "The medium is the message," the subject of the content of the message appeared to be relegated to a place of lesser importance. Recently, however, the pendulum seems to have swung back to giving content more serious consideration. In this section, we present those titles that deal with this topic not only in a broad, general sense, but we also consider titles that deal with the more specific content perspectives of daypart and portrayal.

Three titles deal with broad content overview perspectives: James Miller, *The Social Control of Mass Communication: A Critical Analysis of Content Shaping Forces;* Muriel Cantor, *Prime-Time Television: Content and Control;* and *The Entertainment Functions of Television,* edited by Percy Tannenbaum. The broadest of the three is the Miller book, which explores the implications and consequences of mass communication as a social institution in the context of an advanced industrialized society. Cantor's book, on the other hand, is an introductory analysis of who has control of what we see on television and why. Cantor discusses form and content of prime time TV and the legal and organizational concerns with respect to that control. How the material is produced and what kind of influence the audience may have on TV content and those who control it are also explored. Finally, the prestigious contributors to Tannenbaum's volume look at television's entertainment functions from two broad topic areas: general theoretical speculations and specific content considerations. Employing a variety of methodological and critical tools, the authors relate such concepts as humor, suspense, and violence to the overall vicarious experience of television entertainment.

A number of books focus on specialized areas of TV content. We have selected six titles that deal with daytime television. "Daytime Television: Rhetoric and Ritual," a Ph.D. dissertation by Bernard Timberg, analyzes the network (evening) news, television commercials, and game shows within the broader frameworks of genre and discourse principles. Mary Cassata and Thomas Skill explore American daytime soap operas from the twin perspectives of empirical and humanistic analyses in *Life on Daytime: Tuning-In American Serial Drama.* This study, carried out through Project Daytime, an ongoing research program on daytime serial drama based at The State University of New York at Buffalo, empirically explores character portrayals from such perspectives as psychographics, health, sexual behavior, women, older people, and dyadic interaction. Humanistic approaches focus on family life, soap opera history, fashions, settings, trends, and sociocritical concerns. Muriel Cantor and Suzanne Pingree's *The Soap Opera* presents a reasonable sampling of the literature on soap operas; details the growth and development of soaps on radio and television; and analyzes content, dialogue, and research findings concerning audience characteristics and viewer impact. Michael Intintoli, in *Taking Soaps Seriously: The World of Guiding Light,* produces an ethnographic study that goes behind the scenes and looks at the production of the longest running soap opera, "Guiding Light" (nearly 50 years on radio and TV combined). He presents a wide-ranging chronicle of information, which one would not be likely to find in the published literature. Although not intended for the scholar, *The Soap Opera Book,* by Manuela Soares, stands out as one of the more worthwhile analyses of the soap opera form, its history, content, audience, and social significance. *Soap World,* by Robert La Guardia, written primarily for the popular audience, is of value to the scholar because of its depth of coverage and wealth of detail. The book is divided into three parts: history, complete plot summaries of current soap operas, and an analysis of seven selected past favorites. It fills in many of the blanks for the soap opera researcher who might wish to feel better connected to a serial's history.

In the area of prime time television, Bradley Greenberg, in his book *Life of Television,* examines three years of television drama. The 13 content-analysis studies, carried out by Greenberg and his research associates, are divided into four broad categories: people on television, the sexes, social behaviors, and families on television. According to Greenberg and his team, television's portrayal of people and their social behavior has the potential to influence the value systems and behaviors of viewers of all ages.

In addition to articles on TV content, *Hearth and Home: Images of Women in the Mass Media,* edited by Gaye Tuchman, Arlene Kaplan Daniels, and James Benet, includes material on TV effects, women's magazines, and women's pages in newspapers. While not claiming to be comprehensive, the book is useful as a starting point for those who are interested in the subject of women and the media.

Two additional titles on the portrayals of women in television drama are *Images of Nurses on Television,* by Philip and Beatrice Kalisch and Margaret Scobey, and *Ladies of the Evening: Women Characters of Prime-Time Television,* by Diana Meehan. *Images of Nurses* is an exhaustive historical survey, using quantitative and qualitative methods to describe portrayals primarily on prime time television but includes a chapter on daytime TV as well. The author of *Ladies of the Evening* examines the image of women in a selected number of vintage situation comedies; develops a classification scheme for women types such as "The Good Wife" and "The Imp," complete with a brief description of the corresponding situation comedy; and concludes that the image of women is out of sync with reality.

It is difficult to sidestep distortion and stereotyping in research dealing with television portrayals, and numerous books and studies have made this at least a part of their analyses. Three titles are devoted entirely to this subject. J. Fred MacDonald's *Blacks and White TV: Afro-Americans in Television since 1948* deals with the relative symbolic annihilation perspective. Divided into only three chapters, MacDonald covers (1) TV's unfilled promise of equal opportunity and the removal of the negative stereotypes of Blacks; (2) the treatment of Blacks on TV during the civil rights movement; and (3) the visible, but stereotypical, subordinate role of Blacks after the civil rights movement. *Black Families and the Medium of Television,* edited by Anthony Jackson, has a tripartite focus: (1) it examines the influence of TV images on Black families; (2) it looks at the perspectives of broadcasters in developing those images; and (3) it discusses the role of special interest groups and the federal government in bringing about social change in this area. Randall Miller's *Ethnic Images in American Film and Television* is divided into eight sections of stereotypical treatment of the following ethnic groups: Blacks, Jews, Germans, Irish, Italians and Italian Americans, Poles, Puerto Ricans, and Asians and Asian Americans. Miller raises important questions, but proposals and strategies for corrective action are noticeably absent.

Finally, we cite the book by Jeremy Tunstall, *The Media Are American,* which is the result of a massive research effort by the author, who has examined the media of many countries around the world. His conclusion, that most of the forms and structures as well as their content are American, is a sobering thought.

BIBLIOGRAPHY

Berman, Ronald. *Advertising and Social Change.* Beverly Hills, CA: Sage, 1981.

Blumler, Jay C., and Katz, Elihu, eds. *The Uses of Mass Communication: Current Perspectives on Gratification Research.* Beverly Hills, CA: Sage, 1974.

Bogart, Leo. *The Age of Television: A Study of Viewing Habits and the Impact of Television on American Life.* 3d ed. New York: Ungar, 1972.

Bower, Robert T. *Television and the Public.* New York: Holt, Rinehart, and Winston, 1973.

Brown, Charlene J.; Brown, Trevor R.; and Rivers, William L. *The Media and the People.* New York: Holt, Rinehart, and Winston, 1978.

Cantor, Muriel G. *Prime-Time Television: Content and Control.* Beverly Hills, CA: Sage, 1980.

Cantor, Muriel G., and Pingree, Suzanne. *The Soap Opera.* Beverly Hills, CA: Sage, 1983.

Cassata, Mary, and Skill, Thomas. *Life on Daytime Television: Tuning-In American Serial Drama.* Norwood, NJ: Ablex, 1983.

Chaffee, Steven, and Petrich, Michael J. *Using the Mass Media: Communication Problems in American Society.* New York: McGraw-Hill, 1975.

Clarke, Peter. *New Models for Mass Communication Research.* Beverly Hills, CA: Sage, 1974.

Comstock, George A. *Television in America.* Beverly Hills, CA: Sage, 1980.

Comstock, George A., et al. *Television and Human Behavior.* New York: Columbia University Press, 1978. $B Davis, Dennis K., and Baran, Stanley J. *Mass Communication and Everyday Life: A Perspective on Theory and Effects.* Belmont, CA: Wadsworth, 1981.

Davis, Richard H. *Television and the Aging Audience.* Los Angeles: Ethel Percy Andrus Gerontology Center, University of Southern California, 1980.

Davison, W. Phillips; Boylan, James; and Yu, Frederick T.C. *Mass Media: Systems and Effects.* New York: Praeger, 1976.

Esslin, Martin. *The Age of Television.* San Francisco, CA: W.H. Freeman, 1982.

Frank, Ronald Edward, and Greenberg, Marshall G. *Audiences for Public Television.* Beverly Hills, CA: Sage, 1982.

————. *The Public's Use of Television: Who Watches and Why.* Beverly Hills, CA: Sage, 1980.

Geis, Michael L. *The Language of Television Advertising.* New York: Academic Press, 1982.

Gordon, George. *Erotic Communications: Studies in Sex, Sin and Censorship.* New York: Hastings House, 1980.

Greenberg, Bradley S. *Life on Television: Content Analysis of U.S. TV Drama.* Norwood, NJ: Ablex, 1980.

Greenberg, Bradley S., and Dervin, Brenda. *Uses of the Mass Media by the Urban Poor: Findings of Three Research Projects.* New York: Praeger, 1970.

Greenberg, Bradley S., et al. *Mexican Americans and the Mass Media.* Norwood, NJ: Ablex, 1983.

Hadden, Jeffrey K., and Swann, Charles E. *Prime Time Preachers: The Rising Power of Televangelism.* Reading, MA: Addison-Wesley, 1981.

Hirsch, Paul M.; Miller, Peter V.; and Kline, F. Gerald, eds. *Strategies for Communication Research.* Beverly Hills, CA: Sage, 1977.

Horsfield, Peter. *Religious Television: The Experience in America.* New York: Longman, 1984.

Howitt, Dennis. *The Mass Media and Social Problems.* Oxford, England and Elmsford, NY: Pergamon Press, 1982.

Intintoli, Michael J. *Taking Soaps Seriously: The World of Guiding Light.* New York: Praeger, 1984.

Jackson, Anthony W. *Black Families and the Medium of Television.* Ann Arbor, MI: Bush Program in Child Development and Social Policy, University of Michigan, 1982.

Jacoby, Jacob; Hoyer, Wayne D.; and Sheluga, David A. *Miscomprehension of Televised Communications.* New York: American Association of Advertising Agencies, 1980.

Kalisch, Phillip A.; Kalisch, Beatrice J.; and Scobey, Margaret. *Images of Nurses on Television.* New York: Springer, 1983.

Katz, Elihu. *Mass Media and Social Change.* Beverly Hills, CA: Sage, 1981.

Kline, F. Gerald, and Tichenor, Phillip J. *Current Perspectives in Mass Communication Research.* Beverly Hills, CA: Sage, 1972.

Kressel, Marilyn, ed. *Adult Learning and Public Broadcasting.* Washington, DC: American Association of Community and Junior Colleges, 1980.

La Guardia, Robert. *Soap World.* New York: Arbor House, 1983.

Lemert, James B. *Does Mass Communication Change Public Opinion after All? A New Approach.* Chicago: Nelson-Hall, 1981.

Lerner, Daniel, and Nelson, Lyle M., eds. *Communication Research: A Half-Century Appraisal.* Honolulu, HI: East-West Center, University Press of Hawaii, 1977.

Lowery, Shearon, and DeFleur, Melvin L., eds. *Milestones in Mass Communication Research: Media Effects.* New York: Longman, 1983.

MacDonald, J. Fred. *Blacks and White TV: Afro-Americans in Television since 1948.* Chicago: Nelson-Hall, 1983.

Meehan, Diana M. *Ladies of the Evening: Women Characters of Prime-Time Television.* Metuchen, NJ: Scarecrow, 1983.

Miller, James. *The Social Control of Mass Communication: A Critical Analysis of Content Shaping Forces.* Norwood, NJ: Ablex, 1982.

Miller, Randall N. *Ethnic Images in American Film and Television.* Philadelphia, PA: Balch Institute, 1978.

Pember, Don R. *Mass Media in America.* 3d ed. Chicago: Science Research Associates, 1981.

Primeau, Ronald. *The Rhetoric of Television.* New York: Longman, 1979.

Rice, Ronald E., and Paisley, William J., eds. *Public Communication Campaigns.* Beverly Hills, CA: Sage, 1981.

Salomon, Gavriel. *Interaction of Media, Cognition, and Learning.* San Francisco, CA: Jossey-Bass, 1977.

Schramm, Wilbur Lang, and Roberts, Donald F. *The Process and Effects of Mass Communication.* Rev. ed. Urbana, IL: University of Illinois Press, 1971.

Soares, Manuela. *The Soap Opera Book.* New York: Harmony Books, 1978.

Steiner, Gary Albert. *The People Look at Television: A Study of Audience Attitudes.* New York: Knopf, 1963.

Tannenbaum, Percy H., ed. *The Entertainment Functions of Television.* Sponsored by the Social Science Research Council. Hillsdale, NJ: Lawrence Erlbaum, 1980.

Television and Behavior: Ten Years of Scientific Progress and Implications. 2 vols. Washington, DC: Government Printing Office, 1982.

Timberg, Bernard Mahler. "Daytime Television Rhetoric and Ritual." Ph.D. dissertation. University of Texas, Austin, 1979.

Tuchman, Gaye; Kaplan, Arlene; Benet, James. *Hearth and Home: Images of Women in the Mass Media.* New York: Oxford University Press, 1978.

Tunstall, Jeremy. *The Media are American.* London: Constable; New York: Columbia University Press, 1977.

Withey, Stephen B., and Abeles, Ronald P., eds. *Television and Social Behavior: Beyond Violence and Children.* Hillsdale, NJ: Lawrence Erlbaum, 1980.

Yarrington, Roger. *Using Mass Media for Learning.* Washington, DC: American Association of Community and Junior Colleges, 1979.

Chapter 5
Television Processes and Effects: Children

OVERVIEW

Of all the areas contained within the arena of television, none rival the wealth of research and commentary available on children. The 46 works listed in this chapter attempt to provide the teacher, researcher, and critic with a diversity of perspectives on this controversial and, often, hotly debated topic. Through a blend of both empirical research efforts and critical evaluations, it is our hope to provide the experienced investigator and the novice explorer with the essential resources to synthesize the field, identify its current emphasis, and discover the necessary tools for shaping its future direction.

The subjects of children, television, and violence are so closely enmeshed that the three often defy separation. From the very beginning, researchers have expressed their concern about television's influence on children, and two large-scale studies carried out in 1958 and 1961 respectively probed the violence connection. British researcher Hilde Himmelweit and her colleagues were the first to publish their report, under the title *Television and the Child.* Beginning their report with summaries of their findings and implications and suggestions arising from them, these researchers based their findings on a series of studies of 4,000 children. These studies revealed that the effects of television on children vary with age, sex, intelligence, home background, and personality.

The second large-scale report, published as *Television in the Lives of Our Children* was carried out on the North American continent by Wilbur Schramm, Jack Lyle, and Edwin Parker. This report differs from the Himmelweit study in concept, plan, and raw material. Schramm and his colleagues based their conclusions on a study of 6,000 children and information received from 2,300 parents, teachers, and school officials. Completing 11 studies between 1958 and 1960 in San Francisco, five Rocky Mountain communities, Canada, various American suburbs, and Denver, these researchers took an innovative approach that was to make its mark on virtually all future studies of television and children, for they chose not to ask, "What does television do to children?" but rather, "What do children do with television?" They concluded that "the relationship is always between a kind of television and a kind of child in a kind of situation...that television enters into the whole life of the child...[and that] behind the child there are other relationships of importance—notably with family and friends, school, and church" (p. 169).

Several works issued in the 1970s synthesized information found in hundreds of studies that by then had been carried out on the subject of TV and children. One such work, which appeared in 1973 and was revised in 1982, is *The Early Window,* by Robert Liebert, Joyce Sprafkin, and Emily Davidson. This study synthesized the research on such topics as violence, advertising, social stereotypes, and educational programs. Ray Brown's 1976 compilation, *Children and Television,* attempted to bring together a balanced picture of the research carried out over the previous 20 years. Brown divided his book into three sections: (1) children as an audience, (2) individual and social factors that shape the viewing experience, and (3) processes of influence and some effects of exposures to television. Brown's explanations of what the book does *not* include (e.g., research as to the degree to which children understand television content and the impact of the child's emotional state upon the viewing experience) are perhaps as significant as the actual content in terms of framing the questions future research might address.

Editors Edward Palmer and Aimee Dorr assembled 21 essays in their book *Children and the Faces of Television,* which is divided into three sections: Teaching, Violence, and Selling. Carefully structured, each section parallels the other two in form and balance, with a beginning essay on the historical perspectives of that particular domain and a concluding chapter on future perspectives. In between are chapters focusing on research trends, analysis of content, interpretation of findings, and recommendations for social policy. All in all, the book competently covers a great deal of ground.

In his book *Children in Front of the Small Screen,* Grant Noble makes the observation that the great amount of televiewing that goes on in modern industrial societies must signify that television is fulfilling some fairly basic needs that other mass media before it were apparently unable to satisfy. Therefore, the question "Why is television so popular?" has failed to attract the attention of researchers and consequently has not been fully answered. Noble's thesis is that the varied network of people of different age levels and occupational roles that television presents offers children not only a set of varied perspectives to which they can relate but allows them to be themselves and to interact with the characters and celebrities, rather than lose their identities as they might with characters in cinema films.

Cedric Cullingford, in his work *Children and Television,* has provided readers with a volume that may become an essential bulwark of the field. Cullingford's message is that researchers have failed to come to grips with the nature of the actual "response" to television's "effect." In the tradition of British researchers, Cullingford attempts to dig far beneath the surface, and he raises more questions than the thousands of research studies on this subject have sought to answer. In reporting his own research findings, Cullingford not only masterfully synthesizes much of the previous research but manages also to shatter many of the myths offered as researched generalizations. The book is divided into four main sections: (1) What Children Expect from Television; (2) What Children See in Television: (3) What Children Learn from Television; and (4) What Children Take from Television.

Two final works that set the overview stage are *Children's Television: Economics of Exploitation,* by William Melody, and *What Do TV Producers Know about Their Young Viewers?,* published by Stiftung Prix Jeunesse. Melody reviews the history, economic role, and public policy status of children's television and presents a proposal for ensuring quality and responsibility in children's shows. He calls for the removal of children's television shows from the "commercial" market and the phasing in of external funding to support the programs. Melody's argument for such action is based on his conclusion that as long as commercial interests support these shows, the interest of the child viewer will be supplanted by the vested interests of the advertiser. Taking an opposite approach on this issue are the people associated with the international Prix Jeunesse meetings and seminars. The four studies covered in this book attempt to find out what the producers responsible for creating programs for children think about their audience. These studies inquire into the producers' roles, their tasks and objectives, how they value their work, and what obstacles and problems they perceive in the industry. Through the incorporation of the producers' comments, a survey was conducted that tested how closely the perceptions of the producers matched the way that this specialized audience saw itself.

CRITICAL APPRAISALS

In an effort to explain how children use television and to ultimately provide readers with plans of action for positive "intervention" in the viewing process, writers and commentators within the critical tradition have furnished the field with many useful volumes. A unique work by the people at Action for Children's Television addresses a too often overlooked segment of the television audience, the teenager. Meg Schwartz, as editor, has assembled the thoughts and suggestions of 42 experts from the social sciences and from the industry in *TV & Teens: Experts Look at the Issues.* This compilation addresses such concerns as how teens use television to learn about adulthood and what kinds of programming might be created to assist in this curiosity and includes a number of area analyses—"Role Models," "The World of Work," "Sex and Sexuality," and "Youth in Crisis." Other sections provide background discussions on "The Young Adolescent" and on "TV as Information and Entertainment."

On the proactive side, *The ACT Guide to Children's Television,* by Evelyn Kaye (also from Action for Children's Television), offers a detailed, step-by-step approach which can be employed by parents to assist their children in becoming critical viewers of television. Kaye's premise is that television can become a positive force in young people's lives. Of similar style are two other works: *Teaching Television: How to Use Television to Your Children's Advantage,* by Dorothy Singer, Jerome Singer, and Diana Zuckerman, and *Teaching Television Critical Viewing Skills,* by James Anderson and Milton Ploghoft. Both volumes explore numerous ways in which readers can make the viewing experience meaningful to young audience members. Strategies that emphasize creative applications of program material and methods to encourage discussion and critical thinking about the medium are provided.

Mariann Pezzella Winick and Charles Winick, in *The Television Experience: What Children See,* questioned whether children differ from adults in their reactions to what they see on television. They found that children and adults experience the various aspects of television viewing (i.e., fantasy, believability, identification, humor, morality, and violence) in substantially different ways, suggesting that program popularity may be interpreted in terms of developmental level.

In *Growing Up on Television,* Kate Moody reveals her deep concern over television's impact on children. Moody exhorts parents to take control of the television experience in their children's lives, not by banning television but by exercising judicious control and by melding the vicarious experience it offers with other real-life experiences.

Moody makes a compelling case in her factual presentation and synthesis, arguing that remedial action is needed in order to translate television into a positive experience.

Two books that also advocate a positive approach in utilizing television are *Television and Children,* by Michael Howe, and *Children, Television, and Sex-Role Stereotyping,* by Frederick Williams, et al. Howe, a psychologist, explores the pluses and minuses of television and concludes that equal time and attention should be given to investigating the positive aspects of television's uses for social gain. Williams and his colleagues illustrate this concept by developing the Television Career Awareness Project (TV CAP) to combat sex-role stereotyping in children.

The Plug-In Drug by Marie Winn, a popular writer, deserves inclusion in bibliographies about research dealing with the subject of television's influence on children because of the controversy it has created and the amount of consciousness raising it has engendered. Whatever critics claim the book's demerits to be in terms of Winn's documentation or research methodology, many of her points are, nevertheless, sufficiently provocative to stimulate researchers to look more closely at the way television influences children's cognitive and social development.

SOCIAL EFFECTS

When one thinks of the "social effects" of television, especially where children are concerned, violence tends to come to mind first. While many researchers focus on violence, there still remains a hardy core of people who look beyond this element into areas such as socialization, learning, and nonviolent behavior patterns. Gordon Berry and Claudia Mitchell-Kernan provide an excellent example of this with their book *Television and the Socialization of the Minority Child.* Extensively referenced and well indexed by both author and subject, this book would be a worthy addition to any library. Multidisciplinary in their approach, the authors cover research on television as it relates to Afro-American, Native-American, Hispanic, and Asian-American children. This edited volume has 17 primary contributors who address issues such as cognitive and emotional development in minority children, stereotyping, self-concept, and language socialization. The review and commentary on research focusing on minority children and methodological suggestions on future work will be useful to those interested in conducting investigations in this area.

Two works from researchers in Sweden focus on the socialization aspects of television viewing by adolescents. Elias Hedinsson's *TV, Family and Society: The Social Origins and Effects of Adolescents' TV Use* provides a longitudinal perspective on how adolescents used television over a four-year time period. Emphasis was placed on self-image, family interaction, and viewing styles. This book may be somewhat inaccessible to the novice social scientist because of its heavy emphasis on methodology and statistical applications. *TV Use and Social Interaction in Adolescence,* by Ulla Johnsson-Smaragdi, also employs a longitudinal research method. An important consideration in this work is the interplay of the human development of the individual with the socialization process. In this study, media use proved to be one of the important influences involved in satisfying adolescent needs and gratifications. It was found that as the adolescent went through life changes, media use and gratifications changed also. This study wisely takes into account the cultural context, thereby making comparisons with other societies more meaningful.

Undoubtedly the most massive research endeavor on the social role of television in the lives of American children, *Television and Social Behavior,* prepared variously by researchers John Murray, George Comstock, and Eli Rubenstien, stands out as a fundamental information resource on children and television. This six-volume project was sponsored by the U.S. Surgeon General in 1972 and involved 23 separate research units, which produced 40 technical papers at a total cost of 1.8 million dollars. The extensive nature of these works makes them an essential component of all television scholars' and researchers' libraries.

VIOLENCE

The first reported documentation of TV violence is said to have occurred during the early 1950s when the results of several studies commissioned by the National Association of Educational Broadcasters revealed that one week's monitoring of New York City television channels produced more than 3,400 threats or actual acts of violence for an average of more than six threats or acts per hour. High as this may seem, the average computed for children's programs approached 22.5 threats or acts per hour—more than three times the rate found in television intended for adults. The rates were found to be even higher in children's comedy dramas, by a ratio of six to one.

Despite the passing of three decades, violence remains as firmly ensconced as ever in television drama generally and especially in television directed toward children. Since the early 1950s, there have been seven congressional hearings focusing on the issue of TV violence, which are reported on by Robert K. Baker, et al. in *Mass Media and Violence: A Report to the National Commission on the Causes and Prevention of Violence.* A major demonstration of official concern is the six-volume report of the Surgeon General's Scientific Advisory Committee on Television and Social Behavior, discussed earlier in this chapter (see "Social Effects"). *TV Violence and the Child: The Evolution and Fate of the Surgeon General's Report,* by Douglass Cater and Steven Strickland, traces the growth, development, and impact of the Surgeon General's report from the origins of the concern over TV violence to the conclusions reached by the investigators.

In Great Britain, William Belson has attracted a great deal of attention for his work on TV violence. His book, *Television Violence and the Adolescent Boy,* is based upon the hypothetical-deductive method as a means of responding to the problem of not being able to employ the ideal naturalistic research approach that involves measuring behavior before and after the advent of television in a society. According to Belson, this methodology attempts to study "causes and effects processes in the real life situation" (p. viii). Belson's research methodology has been hailed as a breakthrough, and his most important finding—that "high exposure to television violence increases the degree to which boys engage in serious violence" (p. 520)—once more stirred up strong debate on the relationship between TV violence and social behavior.

Another important work from Great Britain is *Television and Delinquency,* produced by J.D. Halloran, R.L. Brown, and D.C. Chaney. This study compared the television viewing behaviors and consequences of delinquent and nondelinquent young people. These researchers found that there were distinct differences in the ways each group experienced television content. Most important among their findings was the discovery that delinquent youths were more susceptible to television's undesirable influences than the nondelinquent youths.

In *Television, Imagination, and Aggression,* Jerome and Dorothy Singer confront the question of how TV viewing and play compete for a child's time and speculate as to how the two forms of experience may complement each other as part of a child's development.

Employing an experimental research methodology, Stanley Milgram and R. Lance Shotland, in *Television and Anti-Social Behavior,* attempted to test the impact of three different versions of the same episode of "Medical Center" on various viewing groups. This collection of seven studies illustrates the application of experimental designs in television research and underscores the importance of such an approach for exploring the influence of television on human behavior.

David Kenny, in an extensive review of *Television and Aggression: A Panel Study* by J. Ronald Milavsky, Horst H. Stipp, Ronald C. Kessler, and William S. Rubens, calls this book "the most important work to date on the potential harmful effects of television violence." * Milavsky, et al. conducted two major longitudinal studies. Both studies were conducted over a three-year period, with the first one focusing on children in grades three through six. The second study analyzed teenage boys who ranged in age from 13 to 19. Employing some extremely sophisticated methodological and statistical procedures, the authors attempted to discover the strength and direction of violent television programming's influence on their subjects. In their final analysis, Milavsky and his colleagues concluded that television appears to have no harmful effect with regard to aggressive behavior. Kenny, in his review, encourages a conclusion that states "the effect of viewing television violence on aggressive behavior is weak" (p. 181).

Filling an important gap in the literature of televised violence, Willard Rowland, Jr., in *The Politics of TV Violence,* merges the evolution of concern for mediated violence, in terms of its research tradition and the controversy that surrounded it, with public policy uses and concerns. This work reviews the historical Payne Fund Studies, which began in 1928, through to the most recent National Institute on Mental Health report on television and behavior, which appeared in 1982, focusing on the symbolic issues that encompass society's concern over mediated violent behavior.

ADVERTISING

Without question, one of the most volatile issues in terms of the child/television relationship has been that of television advertising. Concern in this area was first evidenced in the early 1960s with the adoption of guidelines by broadcasters in the advertising of toys to children. Since then, this concern has taken many turns, but it essentially groups around four issues: (1) children's exposure to potentially harmful products such as drugs and highly sugared foods; (2) the direct exploitation of the vulnerability of children; (3) children's lack of sophisti-

---

*Journal of Communication, 34(2) (Winter 1984): pp. 176-88.

cation in evaluating deceptive or misleading advertising techniques; and (4) the potentially adverse effects of cumulative exposure on children's values, attitudes, and behavior.

Nine key issues provide the framework for Richard Adler, et al. in *The Effects of Television Advertising on Children.* These issues range from the ability of the child to distinguish between commercials and program content to the relationship of parent-child interactions as a mediating variable to television advertising. In addition to bringing the reader up-to-date on the work that has already been done in the area of TV advertising and children, the book outlines a number of policy recommendations and next steps for research. An added bonus is found in the book's numerous, comprehensible statistical tables; appendices of industry codes and guidelines for children's television advertising; and its excellent, extensive bibliography.

How Children Learn to Buy, by Scott Ward, et al., probes the areas of television and family socialization in terms of how children learn or fail to learn to become intelligent consumers. The authors focus on children's abilities to process information from television advertising; their findings reveal that age differences, rather than sex or social class differences, are the most important distinguishers of consumer behavioral influences. This book is another in a series of recent publications that pay careful attention to the role that cognitive processes actually play rather than infer such processes from the results of research.

June Esserman, as editor of *Television Advertising and Children: Issues, Research and Findings,* argues that many of the published works that deal with the topic of children and advertising are somewhat flawed because they were written in an "atmosphere of accusations and warnings" (p. 7). This volume attempts to provide a serious discussion of the effects of advertising on children within a framework that rejects both the high-powered warnings of impending disaster as well as the industry-motivated defensive postures.

Televised Medicine, Advertising, and Children, by Thomas S. Robertson, John R. Rossiter, and Terry C. Gleason, is the published report of a research effort that attempted to measure the influence of televised medicine advertising on children. The authors found that overall, television advertising has only a limited impact on the attitudes and beliefs that children develop with regard to medications. The cognitive development and experience of the child as he or she grows older appears to counteract the influence of TV ads. However, these researchers found that TV ads did produce a short-term effect on attitudes and beliefs in children.

LEARNING

Whether, and if so, how children learn from television is one of the most contradictory areas of all the mass media. On the one hand, many researchers and scholars in the field believe that a great deal of learning goes on, but unfortunately, these researchers are looking at the learning of antisocial behaviors. On the other hand, others contend that television destroys many of the essential skills necessary for effective learning, such as children's attention skills. In the midst of this chaos, there are a number of excellent books which attempt to address the range and extent of learning that children might acquire from the television viewing experience.

Herta Sturm and Sabine Jorg's *Information Processing by Young Children: Piaget's Theory of Intellectual Development Applied to Radio and Television* compares the effectiveness of the two media in teaching problem-solving skills to young children aged five to seven years. The authors concluded that television accompanied by detailed verbal commentary as opposed to television accompanied by reduced verbal commentary was more effective than radio, providing that the cognitive capacity of the particular age group was taken into account. The authors suggested that further research be conducted into the linking of heavy viewership of young children to the concept of "media literacy"; into exploring more specifically the role of radio; and into determining at what stage, in terms of age and amount of viewing, visual cues might replace verbal cues in the learning process.

An edited book of research studies, which is also grounded in children's cognitive development theory, is Ellen Wartella's *Children Communicating.* This volume has two recurring themes: (1) children communicate at increasing levels of sophistication as they grow older and (2) the studies are based on the theories of cognitive scholars. Harvey Lesser takes a somewhat more prescriptive position. In his work, *Television and the Pre-School Child,* Lesser explores the extent to which television has been effectively utilized for young children, calling for closer collaboration between child psychologists and television production personnel.

Children's Understanding of Television: Research on Attention and Comprehension, edited by Jennings Bryant and Daniel Anderson, looks at the complex nature of the interaction children have with television. The book begins with an exploration of attention and perception, moves on to examine comprehension, and then provides insight into the application and intervention process. This work takes a solid research approach and is punctuated with serious analysis and in-depth discussion.

Recognizing that television is and will remain an influential force in our society, Milton Ploghoft and James A. Anderson, *Education for the Television Age,* have assembled works from a national conference focusing, for the most part, on the positive use of television in educating children. This collection of 23 papers looks at such elements as receivership skills, nationwide and community involvement activities, the role and process of educational innovation, and the application of a critical televiewing skills curriculum.

CONTENT

The preschool child and television have preoccupied the attention of researchers for a number of years. *Sesame Street* and cognitive development theory have provided a number of rich insights into how television and the young interact. Gerald Lesser provides a positive assessment of and gives the history of thinking behind *Sesame Street* in his book, *Children and Television,* while Thomas Cook and his colleagues take a more critical look in their book, *"Sesame Street" Revisited.* They turn up evidence that *Sesame Street* may not have caused the large learning gains initially claimed, and they wonder whether the "right" children are being benefited.

In a more descriptive fashion, Joseph Turow's *Entertainment, Education, and the Hard Sell* and F. Earle Barcus's *Children's Television: An Analysis of Programming and Advertising* offer similar perspectives on children's television. Turow's book was undertaken when he realized that the data he had collected for another study (commissioned by the FCC on series programming for children on the three networks, 1948–1978) suggested themes of "diversity" and "shape." Massaging this data, Turow wrote his book showing that diversity in children's series programming occurred in stages, through a complex mixture of changes in scheduling, subject matter, format, and characterization. Although his primary focus is on programming, Turow has also delineated the environment surrounding the programming, exploring the influences that have affected its direction and nature. Barcus's content analysis study of weekend and weekday afternoon commercial television was also carried out to objectively assess the changes occurring in children's television programs and also to explore advertising themes and formats; the incidence of aggressive behavior; and the descriptions of racial, cultural, and sexual representations.

Extending his earlier work into the realm of sex-role, minority, and family portrayals, Barcus has given the field a valuable book,

Images of Life on Children's Television, which takes as its basic premise that children do learn from their environment. He then explores the potential impact of such subjects as sex-roles, minorities, and the family within the context of TV portrayals in programs directed at children.

A comprehensive reference work on children's animated cartoon series is George Woolery's *Children's Television: The First Thirty-Five Years, 1946–1981. Part I: Animated Cartoon Series.* This volume provides descriptive information on some 300 network and syndicated programs, listed in alphabetical order.

Chronicling the development, implementation, production, and evaluation of a television series designed to break through the stereotypes found in children's TV shows is the focus of Jerome Johnson and James Ettema's book *Positive Images: Breaking Stereotypes with Children's Television.* The authors discuss the process whereby creative TV personnel, educators, and researchers combined efforts to create *Freestyle,* a PBS children's program, and how its impact on children was carefully measured and evaluated. This work may well serve as the model for planned prosocial television programming in the future.

BIBLIOGRAPHY

Adler, Richard, et al., eds. *The Effects of Television Advertising on Children: Review and Recommendations.* Lexington, MA: Heath, 1980.

Anderson, James A., and Ploghoft, Milton E. *Teaching Critical Television Viewing Skills: An Integrated Approach.* Springfield, IL: Thomas, 1982.

Baker, Robert K., et al. *Mass Media and Violence: A Report to the National Commission on the Causes and Prevention of Violence.* Washington, DC: Government Printing Office, 1969.

Barcus, F. Earle. *Children's Television: An Analysis of Programming and Advertising.* New York: Praeger, 1977.

––––––. *Images of Life on Children's Television: Sex Roles, Minorities, and Families.* New York: Praeger, 1983.

Belson, William A. *Television Violence and the Adolescent Boy.* Farnborough, UK: Saxon House, 1978.

Berry, Gordon L, and Mitchell-Kernan, Claudia, eds. *Television and the Socialization of the Minority Child.* Chicago: Academy Press, 1982.

Brown, Ray, ed. *Children and Television.* Beverly Hills, CA: Sage, 1976.

Bryant, Jennings, and Anderson, Daniel, eds. *Children's Understanding of Television: Research on Attention and Comprehension.* New York: Academic Press, 1983.

Cater, Douglass, and Strickland, Stephen, eds. *TV Violence and the Child: The Evolution and Fate of the Surgeon General's Report.* New York: Russell Sage Foundation, 1975.

Cook, Thomas D., et al. *"Sesame Street" Revisited.* New York: Russell Sage Foundation, 1975.

Cullingford, Cedric. *Children and Television.* New York: St. Martin's Press, 1984.

Esserman, June. *Television Advertising and Children: Issues Research and Findings.* New York: New York Children Research Service, 1981.

Halloran, J.D.; Brown, R.L.; and Chaney, D.C. *Television and Delinquency.* Atlantic Highlands, NJ: Humanities Press, 1970.

Hedinsson, Elias. *TV, Family, and Society: The Social Origins and Effects of Adolescents' TV Use.* Stockholm, Sweden: Almquist & Wiksell, 1981.

Himmelweit, Hilde T., et al. *Television and the Child: An Empirical Study of the Effects of Television on the Young.* New York: Oxford University Press, 1958.

Howe, Michael. *Television and Children.* Hamden, CT: Shoe String Press, 1977.

Jeunesse, Prix. *What Do TV Producers Know about their Young Viewers?* New York: K.G. Saur, 1979.

Johnson, Jerome, and Ettema, James. *Positive Images: Breaking Stereotypes with Children's TV.* Beverly Hills, CA: Sage, 1982.

Johnsson-Smaragdi, Ulla. *TV Use and Social Interaction in Adolescence: A Longitudinal Study.* Stockholm, Sweden: Almquist & Wiksell, 1983.

Kaye, Evelyn. *The ACT Guide to Children's Television: Or How to Treat TV With T.L.C.* Rev. ed. Boston: Beacon Press, 1979.

Lesser, Gerald S. *Children and Television: Lessons from "Sesame Street."* New York: Random House, 1974.

Lesser, Harvey. *Television and the Preschool Child: A Psychological Theory of Instructional and Curriculum Development.* New York: Academic Press, 1977.

Liebert, Robert M.; Sprafkin, Joyce; and Davidson, Emily. *The Early Window: Effects of Television on Children and Youth.* Rev. ed. Elmsford, NY: Pergamon, 1982.

Melody, William. *Children's Television: Economics of Exploitation.* New Haven, CT: Yale University Press, 1973.

Milavsky, J. Ronald, et al. *Television and Aggression: A Panel Study.* New York: Academic Press, 1982.

Milgram, Stanley, and Shotland, R. Lance. *Television and Anti-Social Behavior.* New York: Academic Press, 1973.

Moody, Kate. *Growing Up on Television. The TV Effect: A Report to Parents.* New York: Times Books, 1980.

Murray, John P.; Rubenstein, Eli A.; and Comstock, George, eds. *Television and Social Behavior: A Technical Report to the Surgeon General's Scientific Advisory Committee on Television and Social Behavior.* Vol. 1. *Media Content and Control;* Vol. 2. *Television and Social Learning;* Vol. 3. *Television and Adolescent Aggressiveness;* Vol 4. *Television in Day-to-Day Life: Patterns of Use;* Vol. 5. *Television's Effects: Further Explorations;* Vol. 6. *Television and Growing Up: The Impact of Televised Violence.* Washington, DC: Government Printing Office, 1972.

Noble, Grant. *Children in Front of the Small Screen.* Beverly Hills, CA: Sage, 1975.

Palmer, Edward, and Dorr, Aimee, eds. *Children and the Faces of Television: Teaching, Violence, Selling.* New York: Academic Press, 1980.

Ploghoft, Milton E., and Anderson, James A., eds. *Education for the Television Age: The Proceedings of a National Conference on the Subject of Children and Television.* Springfield, IL: C.C. Thomas, 1981.

Robertson, Thomas S.; Rossiter, John R.; and Gleason, Terry C. *Televised Medicine, Advertising, and Children.* New York: Praeger, 1980.

Rowland, Willard, Jr. *The Politics of TV Violence.* Beverly Hills, CA: Sage, 1983.

Schramm, Wilbur L.; Lyle, Jack; and Parker, Edwin B. *Television in the Lives of Our Children.* Stanford, CA: Stanford University Press, 1961.

Schwartz, Meg. *TV & Teens: Experts Look at the Issues.* Reading, MA: Addison-Wesley, 1982.

Singer, Dorothy G.; Singer, Jerome; and Zuckerman, Diana. *Teaching Television: How to Use TV to Your Children's Advantage.* New York: Dial, 1981.

Singer, Jerome L., and Singer, Dorothy G. *Television, Imagination, and Aggression: A Study of Preschoolers' Play and Television Viewing Patterns.* Hillsdale, NJ: Lawrence Erlbaum, 1980.

Sturm, Herta, and Jorg, Sabine. *Information Processing by Young Children: Piaget's Theory of Intellectual Development Applied to Radio and Television.* New York: K.G. Saur, 1979.

Turow, Joseph. *Entertainment, Education, and the Hard Sell: Three Decades of Network Children's Television.* New York: Praeger, 1981.

Ward, Scott, et al. *How Children Learn to Buy: The Development of Consumer Information Processing Skills.* Beverly Hills, CA: Sage, 1977.

Wartella, Ellen, ed. *Children Communicating: Media and Development of Thought, Speech, Understanding.* Beverly Hills, CA: Sage, 1979.

Williams, Frederick; LaRose, Robert; and Frost, Frederica. *Children, Television, and Sex-Role Stereotyping.* New York: Praeger, 1981.

Winick, Mariann Pezzella, and Winick, Charles. *The Television Experience: What Children See.* Beverly Hills, CA: Sage, 1979.

Winn, Marie. *The Plug-In Drug.* New York: Viking, 1977.

Woolery, George W. *Children's Television: The First Thirty-Five Years, 1946–81. Part I: Animated Cartoons.* Metuchen, NJ: Scarecrow, 1983.

Chapter 6
Television News

OVERVIEW

Whether it is the take-off of the space shuttle, the landing of released hostages, the assassination or near assassination of world and national leaders, the pageantry of royal or soap opera weddings (the nuptials of *General Hospital's* Luke and Laura were covered by the news media), or the vying for and transfer of presidential power, Americans have developed an ever- increasing appetite for news. Television has sensed this and countered with live, extended coverage of national and international events and crises. In addition, early-morning and late-night network television news shows have become ratings battlegrounds for a new audience of upscale, information-eager viewers. Local stations are rapidly expanding early-evening news programs from 30 to 60 minutes. The infamous "prime time access" slot (the one-hour period in the evening just before network programs begin) is being transformed from the inanity of game shows and boredom of reruns into feature and "lifestyle" news shows such as *PM Magazine* and *Entertainment Tonight.* On cable television, news is given even greater emphasis with *Cable News Network,* an around-the-clock comprehensive news service from Turner Broadcasting Systems, and *C-Span,* which features live, gavel-to-gavel coverage of the U.S. House of Representatives.

Annually since 1963, Roper has reported that the majority of Americans obtain most of their news from television. Since 1961, Americans have been naming TV as the most believable news medium, outstripping newspapers since 1968 by a two-to-one margin. These two points underscore the importance of comprehensive analysis and criticism of the role television news plays in American society.

A number of works present useful overviews of the news environment. Ben H. Bagdikian's *The Information Machines* perceptively analyzes how information and news have evolved in American society. Bagdikian explores the influence of various technologies, politics, and business on the nature and direction of news and information. The historical tracing of news through print to broadcast systems prepares the reader for many insightful comments and criticisms on the future of news and information in society and its impact upon indivduals.

The 13 original papers that appear in Elie Abel's *What's News: The Media in American Society* cover a broad range of issues while also providing a good deal of insight into the news process. Topics include a review of media history, the economics of the news industry, the press and First Amendment relationship, and ownership structures. Political images in network news coverage, media accountability, and the impact of news from a social and cultural perspective are also explored.

John Hartley, in his work *Understanding News*, analyzes news from a semiological perspective (the social meaning of signs and symbols). While primarily British in its examples, this book serves as an important contribution to the understanding of the role of news in American society as well. Hartley addresses the definitional aspects of news, what functions it serves in society, and how we draw meaning from it. This work will provide the reader with the essential tools necessary for critically interpreting the role and influence of the news industry.

NEWS CONTENT

Television Network News: Issues in Content Research, edited by William Adams and Fay Schreibman, is a superb overview of the current research, methods, and direction of television news. This work explores the multifaceted issues that surround research on news content. It places in perspective commentary on current and previous research, analyzes the methodologies employed, and speculates on future approaches in the study of television news.

Providing transcripts of each episode aired during the 1979–1980 television season, CBS's *60 Minutes Verbatim* presents a panoramic view of the subjects covered on the program. Providing an interesting perspective into the organization and structure of the interviews on *60 Minutes,* this collection serves as a valuable record of what one organization deemed newsworthy in that particular year.

Having collected his data through participant observation, Herbert Gans, in his book *Deciding What's News,* presents a fascinating and incisive analysis of four news organizations: *CBS Evening News, NBC Nightly News, Newsweek,* and *TIME.* Gans probes the hows, whats, whys, and whos of news selection and deselection and methods of reporting.

Content analysis of over 4,000 news stories which appeared on the three major networks was used as the basis for C. Richard Hofstetter's work *Bias in the News: Network Television News Coverage of the 1972 Election Campaign.* While this book tries to answer the question of whether or not there is an identifiable bias in coverage of elections, and if so, whether it is politically motivated or structurally designed, this work serves as an excellent resource on political news content as well.

Although *Bad News,* which is the result of a detailed study by the Glasgow University Media Group, focuses primarily on the British television news operations, it offers many lessons to the American news observer. In both the U.S. and Britain, news consumers indicate that television is their most common and most believable source of news. The *Bad News* analysis showed that television news favors certain individuals by giving them more time and status, a conclusion not posited lightly, for the researchers carefully demonstrate the procedures employed in coding and analyzing the data. A second volume by the same group, *More Bad News,* presents detailed case studies and analyzes them, using the techniques developed in the first volume. Both books would be useful from a methodological as well as from an analytical orientation.

SOCIAL ROLE AND IMPACT

"A picture is worth a thousand words" and "Seeing is believing" are among those enduring pronouncements that people more readily believed before the Age of Television. Now, that is not so. It comes as no surprise to the critics that TV's "happy talk" news programs, more than any other area of programming, are being held responsible for this new skepticism. In Chapter 2, we cited Erik Barnouw's *Tube of Plenty* as an important work focusing on the growth of television and its influence on American life. Comparing TV news to radio news, Barnouw wrote: "A favorite pronouncement of the day was that television had added a 'new dimension' to newscasting. The truth of this concealed a more serious fact: the camera, as arbiter of news value, had introduced a drastic curtailment of the scope of news....Analysis, a staple of radio news in its finest days, was being shunted aside as non-visual" (p. 169).

It appeared that the die had been cast: visualness was equated to entertainment; smooth-flowing delivery, preplanned for visual interest, became more important than content. The pseudoevent—all too often covered by "Eyewitness News" teams whose "on the spot coverage," according to critics such as Stanley Baran, in *The Viewer's Television Book,* is carefully "designed to make us believe that what we are seeing is the way it is—is daily discussed by newscasters with nary a hair of their well-coiffured heads out of place. These elements, combined with voice-overs, edited cuts, time and placement decisions, and supplementary visuals, produce a representation of the news, not an eyewitness account" (p. 87). The dean of newscasters, Walter Cronkite, described in a 1976 convention of radio and television news directors, the most serious problem of television news as the inevitable distortion resulting from the hypercompression of trying to force-fit 100 pounds of news into a one-pound sack for the nightly news broadcast, during which the public was hit with a series of "blivets."

Robert Rutherford Smith, in *Beyond the Wasteland,* developed a list of recent and current issues of broadcast news that he felt suggested the kinds of issues to be faced in the future. In addition to those we have already cited, Smith listed the influences of controlling corporate interests; the biases of reporters, producers, and writers; the overemphasis on bad news; news "management" by skilled public officials; and the influence of "show business" recommendations of news consultants. Suggesting a number of standards to be used as starting points to overcome broadcasting criticisms, Smith posed a number of questions to be applied to the news genre, including the following: Does the reporter compensate for personal biases? Is the reporting balanced or one-sided? Are the events suggested for inclusion significant?

How and why do certain events get selected as news? What models of presentation and what underlying models of deviance and social problems are employed in the media? How do these elements influence our conceptions of social problems in society and what effect does this have on groups designated as "socially problematic?" These questions form the basis of *The Manufacture of News: Social Problems, Deviance, and the Mass Media,* edited by Stanley Cohen and Jock Young, which attempts to grapple with the sociological implications of news selection, presention, and consequences.

David Altheide's study of television news, entitled *Creating Reality,* attempts to assess the current state of news practices. Taking a position similar to Cohen and Young's, Altheide charges the nightly newscasts with distorting what they claim to represent and, in the process, adding to our social problems. He traces the foundations of what he terms the "news perspective"—which is a convoluted way of simplifying events—to the external forces of commercialism, scheduling, technology, and competition. Throughout his study, Altheide suggests solutions and possible ways to defensively scrutinize the distorted news messages. In our opinion, the analyses of Cohen and Young and Altheide represent the best in attempts to understand the role news plays in setting the "social agenda" in contemporary society.

The ethical problems of the news media are explored by John Hulteng. In *The Messenger's Motives,* he skillfully analyzes and comments on more than 150 cases involving media ethics, questioning the impact of the decisions that were made. Robert Cirino, in a similar effort, has compiled a valuable work entitled *Power to Persuade,* which consists of over 150 case studies dealing with the problems of objectivity, censorship, conflict of interest, and the "free marketplace of ideas." The case studies themselves make fascinating reading, but with each one accompanied by a list of possible activities and relevant questions for discussion, the book achieves a virtually limitless potential for use in media or journalism courses. In *The Newscasters,* Ron Powers explores the conflict between the pursuit of high ratings and responsible reporting by using various news personalities as case studies to demonstrate an increasing trend toward "show-biz" news. From a different perspective, Edward Jay Epstein explores the organizational structure of the three network news operations in his book *News from Nowhere.* He investigates the internal and external political and economic factors that influence the news selection process and, in his well-argued conclusion, questions the widely held industry position that TV news mirrors and informs the public.

Stephan Lesher, in his work *Media Unbound: The Impact of Television Journalism on the Public,* makes a rather comprehensive analysis of the media's news function. Armed with numerous examples of how the news media in general, and television in particular, failed to do its job, Lesher argues that in many cases both mistaken and distorted reporting has caused serious misperceptions on the part of the public. The implication of these "manipulations" can be seen within the context of Lesher's examples.

The manipulative aspects of the media are approached from a different angle in *The Interplay of Influence: Mass Media and Their Publics in News, Advertising, and Politics,* by Kathleen Hall Jamieson and Karlyn Kohrs Campbell. These authors contend that the media are manipulated by a broad range of external and internal elements. These influences, which cover both the day-to-day pressures of surviving in a competitive industry, as well as the more pervasive sociocultural aspects, are ultimately passed on to the consuming audience. The impact of this process is discussed at length.

INTERNATIONAL PERSPECTIVES AND COVERAGE

Americans suffer from a geocentric world view. This tendency to perceive events, and the locus of control, as emanating from the United States has often been attributed to the fact that the news and information upon which we make our judgments is almost completely American in both its source and interpretation. What is the significance of such a narrow perspective? How does it color our perceptions of other nations and other cultures? What impact does this have on other people's perceptions of Americans? These are just a few of many important questions that arise concerning international news coverage.

William C. Adams found in his work, *Television Coverage of International Affairs,* that news reporting of world events was most often presented in terms of its link to U.S. interests, overlooking the more important implications of the event. Other elements addressed by Adams include the overemphasis on news that has high visual interest but may not be all that significant in other aspects. He comments on the "formulaic" approach to putting together a news story and contends that it may create an inaccurate impression of nonindustrialized societies.

In another work edited by Adams, *Television Coverage of the Middle East,* a combination of content analysis and interview techniques are employed to address the issue of how the American news media both reports and ignores Middle East news events and what the implication of this selection process has upon viewers' understanding of Middle East affairs. This book stands out as a unique contribution based on its wealth of research, which focuses on a very important, but often understudied international community.

Crises in International News, edited by Jim Richstad and Michael Anderson, explores the process and impact of international information flow between industrialized and developing nations. This book provides an excellent analysis of the ongoing debate over the nature, access, and control of news and information throughout the world. *Making the News,* by Peter Golding and Philip Elliott, offers a three-country perspective on broadcast news operations. The authors investigate the production and content of news in Nigeria, Sweden, and Ireland in an attempt to answer two basic research questions: What picture of the world is provided by broadcast news? and How is this picture related to the routine demands of news production in broadcasting organizations? Although this specific study focuses on three countries only, the fundamental questions and issues raised by the authors are timely and relevant to all societies.

CRITICAL APPRAISALS

Often the news media in open societies are characterized as the eyes of the people and conscience of government. A common retort to this perspective is "Who watches the news media?" The response to this may very well be "The news critics." Should this prove to be true, then we, as the "people" can rest easy because this is one area where there is no shortage of critical interpretation and prescription. Most outstanding in this field are the eight volumes edited by Marvin Barrett, which have been sponsored almost yearly since 1968 by the Alfred I. DuPont Foundation. These works, each published under a separate title and subheaded as *The Alfred I. Dupont-Columbia University Survey of Broadcast Journalism,* represent what may be the best single collection of television news criticism and analysis available in the United States. Contributors to these volumes range from industry insiders and friendly foes to government legislators and hard-line idealists. Each volume of this survey provides an integrated review of the major issues, controversies, and significant happenings of the year in news; a comprehensive and balanced interpretation of the news media's performance; and provocative essays on the current directions and future challenges of the industry.

Edwin Diamond and his News Study Group at the Massachusetts Institute of Technology have produced three works that rival the efforts of Marvin Barrett. As one of the most astute observers of the television news scene, Diamond, in *The Tin Kazoo: Good News, Bad News* and *Sign Off: The Last Days of Television,* provides invaluable insights into the relationship of news and politics with television. Diamond's blend of case studies, news and political analysis, and audience role is offered with careful commentary, making these works required reading for all students of the media.

Criticism and analysis by news industry insiders generally moves in one of two directions: perspectives that demonstrate how those inside think and perform and perspectives that provide solid analysis and recommendations with the added insight of how things really happen. An example of the first can be found in a book by Av Westin entitled *Newswatch: How TV Decides the News.* Westin, who is currently affiliated with ABC TV's *20/20* program, offers a good deal of information on the "culture" of the news industry, explicating the role and impact of individuals and organizations on the news collecting and dissemination process at the network level. Bob Teague's *Live and Off-Color: News Biz,* while written with humor, should not be discounted. Teague takes his craft seriously and posits a number of suggestions which he feels will bring some integrity back to local news coverage. His analysis thoroughly outlines the major problems that an overly competitive ratings race has created. It may be difficult to implement his solutions, but they may initiate overdue discussions about how to responsibly and effectively communicate news to the local public.

While the issue of news bias is ever present in all critical analyses of news event coverage, Edith Efron, in her work *The News Twisters,* lays out a comprehensive case of bias against the three television networks' coverage of events surrounding the 1968 presidential election. Her prime thesis is that network coverage has an overt left-wing bias. Best read in conjunction with this work is Efron's follow-up analysis of efforts by CBS to discredit her, which is entitled *How CBS Tried to Kill a Book.* This volume discusses the measures that CBS took to make Efron appear equally biased and methodologically naive in her analysis of the news and charges against it.

On the other side of the coin, William E. Porter, in *Assault on the Media,* traces over five years of efforts by the Nixon administration to "intimidate, harass, regulate, and in other ways damage the news media in their functioning as part of the American political system" (p. vii). Valuable both for the historical record it presents as well as for the still burning issues it articulates, the book chronologically follows those efforts from 1969 to 1974 and concludes with a discussion of the effects upon news operations.

BIBLIOGRAPHY

Abel, Elie, ed. *What's News: The Media in American Society.* San Francisco, CA: Institute for Contemporary Studies, 1981.

Adams, William C., ed. *Television Coverage of International Affairs.* Norwood, NJ: Ablex 1982.

———. *Television Coverage of the Middle East.* Norwood, NJ: Ablex, 1981.

Adams, William C., and Schreibman, Fay, eds. *Television Network News: Issues in Content Research.* Washington, DC: George Washington University, 1978.

Altheide, David L. *Creating Reality: How TV News Distorts Events.* Beverly Hills, CA: Sage, 1976.

Bagdikian, Ben H. *The Information Machines: Their Impact on Men and the Media.* New York: Harper & Row, 1971.

Baran, Stanley J. *The Viewer's Television Book: A Personal Guide to Understanding Television and Its Influence.* Cleveland, OH: Penrith, 1980.

Barrett, Marvin, ed. *The Alfred I. DuPont-Columbia University Survey of Broadcast Journalism.* Vol. 1 *Survey of Broadcast Journalism, 1968–1969.* New York: Gossett & Dunlap, 1969; Vol. 2 *Survey of Broadcast Journalism, 1969–1970: Year of Challenge, Year of Crisis.* New York: Gossett & Dunlap, 1970; Vol. 3 *Survey of Broadcast Journalism, 1970–1971: A State of Siege.* New York: Gossett & Dunlap, 1971; Vol. 4 *The Politics of Broadcasting, 1970–1972.* New York: Crowell, 1973; Vol. 5 *Moments of Truth?* New York: Crowell, 1975; Vol.6 *Rich News, Poor News.* New York: Crowell, 1978; Vol. 7 *The Eye of the Storm.* New York: Lippincott & Crowell, 1980; Vol. 8 *Broadcast Journalism, 1979–1981* New York: Dodd, Mead, An Everest House Book, 1982.

CBS, Inc. CBS News. *60 Minutes Verbatim.* New York: Arno, 1980.

Cirino, Robert. *Power to Persuade: Mass Media and the News.* New York: Bantam Books, 1974.

Cohen, Stanley, and Young, Jock, eds. *The Manufacture of News: Deviance, Social Problems and the Mass Media.* Rev. ed. Beverly Hills, CA: Sage, 1981.

Diamond, Edwin. *Good News, Bad News.* Cambridge, MA: MIT Press, 1978.

———. *Sign Off: The Last Days of Television.* Cambridge, MA: MIT Press, 1982.

———. *The Tin Kazoo: Politics, Television, and the News.* Cambridge, MA: MIT Press, 1975.

Efron, Edith. *How CBS Tried to Kill a Book.* Los Angeles: Nash, 1972.

———. *The News Twisters.* Los Angeles: Nash, 1971.

Epstein, Edward Jay. *News from Nowhere: Television and the News.* New York: Random House, 1973.

Gans, Herbert J. *Deciding What's News: A Study of CBS Evening News, NBC Nightly News, Newsweek, and Time.* New York: Pantheon, 1979.

Glasgow University Media Group. *Bad News.* Boston: Routledge & Kegan Paul, 1976.

———. *More Bad News.* Boston: Routledge & Kegan Paul, 1980.

Golding, Peter, and Elliott, Philip. *Making the News.* New York: Longman, 1979.

Hartley, John. *Understanding News.* New York: Methuen, 1982.

Hofstetter, C. Richard. *Bias in the News: Network Television Coverage of the 1972 Election Campaign.* Columbus, OH: Ohio State University Press, 1972.

Hulteng, John L. *The Messenger's Motives: Ethical Problems of the News Media.* Englewood Cliffs, NJ: Prentice-Hall, 1976.

Jamieson, Kathleen H., and Campbell, Karlyn K. *The Interplay of Influence: Mass Media & Their Publics in News, Advertising, Politics.* Belmont, CA: Wadsworth, 1983.

Lesher, Stephan. *Media Unbound: The Impact of Television Journalism on the Public.* Boston: Houghton-Mifflin, 1982.

Porter, William E. *Assault on the Media: The Nixon Years.* Ann Arbor, MI: University of Michigan Press, 1976.

Powers, Ron. *The Newscasters: The News Business as Show Business.* Rev ed. New York: St Martin's Press, 1980.

Richstad, Jim, and Anderson, Michael. *Crisis in International News: Policies & Prospects.* New York: Columbia University Press, 1981.

Smith, Robert Rutherford. *Beyond the Wasteland: The Criticism of Broadcasting.* Annandale, VA: Speech Communication Association, 1976.

Teague, Bob. *Live and Off-Color: News Biz.* New York: A & W Publishers, 1982.

Westin, Av. *Newswatch: How TV Decides the News.* New York: Simon & Schuster, 1982.

Chapter 7
Television and Politics

OVERVIEW

The marriage of politics and the mass media has been one of the most enduring alliances in American history. Very early, American politicians went to the media with more understanding than most of us have had going to the polls. First newspapers, then radio, and now television have been harnessed by politicos as natural assets for attaining their politicl goals. Unfortunately, as media technology has moved forward, political progress as assessed in the media has seemed to move backward from the arena of issues and substance to that of image and fluff.

No one can deny, for instance, that in the televised 1960 presidential campaign debates, Nixon's haggard appearance, capped by a heavy growth of "five o'clock shadow," tipped the 1960 election scales in favor of the more alert, clean-cut Kennedy. The point has been repeatedly made that today's candidates are not so much measured against their political predecessors—the Roosevelts, Trumans, and Eisenhowers—as they are against today's television entertainment personalities—Johnny Carson, Phil Donahue, and Dick Cavett. It has even been hinted that the reason the Republican party—at a time when it badly needed to improve its image—chose smooth, polished, actor-politician Ronald Reagan as its standard-bearer was that he had been trained all his life to be a showman. Whatever their personal politics might be, it seems clear that all Americans must heighten their awareness of political massaging of the media to mislead voters into thinking that clever campaigners equate with competent office holders.

This, of course, is only one aspect of the media's influence in political life. Its ability to inform the public, to expose corruption, to shape public opinion, to set the agenda, and to socialize us politically are but a few of the other aspects to be considered. We have selected materials that we believe present perceptive analyses of the role the mass media, particularly television, play in politics.

The Effects of Mass Communication on Political Behavior, by Sidney Kraus and Dennis Davis, is a comprehensive overview of the field of political communication and the role mass communication plays in it. The authors begin with a discussion of political socialization followed by an examination of the media's influence on the election process, the dissemination of political information, and how people use the media in the political process. They continue with an assessment of how political reality is constructed in society and conclude with political communication research methods and a summation of conclusions. An excellent companion text, *Political Communication,* edited by Steven Chaffee, focuses on the research horizons in political communication, giving special emphasis to linking theoretical perspectives to the various research strategies.

While direct effects investigations have proved to be unsuccessful in almost every area of mass communication research, Michael MacKuen and Steven Coombs, in *More than News: Media Power in Public Affairs,* have found a good deal of evidence to support this notion when it is studied from the "agenda setting" perspective. This book, which is essentially two distinct studies, explores this effects position and posits two models of how this influence operates on individuals.

Media, Power, Politics, a highly readable and well-documented work by David Paletz and Robert Entman, is divided into three parts. Beginning with a discussion of power in America and how it relates to the media, followed by an analysis of the "media manipulators" (this term includes the candidates, presidents, Congress, courts, law enforcers, and interest groups), the book next looks at the "manipulated public," focusing on public opinion and how it is influenced. In a more specific vein and spanning a much broader political arena than works previously mentioned, Anne Rawley Saldich investigates television's impact on the American political process in her book *Electronic Democracy.* The author discusses the social role of television in the political process, the nature of power and credibility in mediated politics, the decision-making and gatekeeping processes that limit or control access to the media, as well as the ways in which politicians and pressure groups have tried to manipulate television coverage to their own benefit. This is an interesting and unique work in that it demonstrates the inseparability of power from media in America.

An excellent overview of political communication research can be found in Robert Meadow's *Politics as Communication.* This well-referenced work also proposes a model of political communication theory and process and effectively demonstrates the application of communication research techniques in the political science arena. This extremely comprehensive book probes the political dimensions of language, culture, and symbols, affording the reader many avenues through which to integrate politics and communication with people and society.

Broadly based and unique in its approach, *Mediated Political Realities,* by Dan Nimmo and James Combs, explores the political dimensions of mass communication and how it shapes our public understanding of society. In a series of critical chapters, the authors analyze and discuss a wide variety of topics from political values in film and pop culture in television to news coverage of political campaigns and the political power of professional sports. In other sections, Nimmo and Combs extend their arguments into the realm of melodrama as an interpreter of social reality. Taking a more traditional approach, Doris Graber, in *Mass Media and American Politics,* reviews the state of research and provides useful examples of the interrelationship of politics and the media. Topical areas such as voting, press coverage of international news events, the influence of campaign coverage on voter attitudes and behavior, and the shaping and reinforcement power of the media as well as the agenda-setting role the media play are thoroughly discussed and well argued.

The Communications Revolution in Politics, edited by Gerald Benjamin, focuses on an important new area of political communication—the role and influence of new technologies. Advances in public opinion polling, increased sophistication in utilizing television, the regulation of communication systems and their impact on politics and policy, and the issue of privacy are just a few of the essay topics presented in this volume.

Sig Mickelson addresses the issue of how television has influenced the U.S. political system both domestically and abroad in his work *The Electric Mirror: Politics in an Age of Television.* Employing a historical approach which covers TV and politics from the 1950s through the early 1970s, Mickelson draws on his own personal experiences as one-time president of CBS News. His research is solid and his arguments are well founded. Taking the position that television has altered the political landscape through its demand for visualness and action, Austin Ranney, in *Channels of Power: The Impact of Television on American Politics,* explores the ways in which the television industry must voluntarily come to grips with its excessive influence on the structure and process of the political system in the United States.

CAMPAIGNS AND ADVERTISING

"Posing for Office," the title of a chapter in *Media Made in California,* by British researchers Jeremy Tunstall and David Walker, seems to be a singularly apt descriptor of present-day politics in the U.S., as in many countries of the world. Tunstall and Walker describe the Hollywood/political connection in the following words: "Hollywood has given California politics three kinds of gifts: former actors turned politicians, media skills to be put to use in politics, and a version of celebrity as a universal quality to be transferred between screen and hustings at will" (p. 174). Despite the Hollywood connection that these authors so perceptively describe, neither they nor other observers of the political scene foresee political campaign tactics as undergoing much change in the near future. The political spot announcements—the "blivets" of the American political environment—will still persist.

Jeff Greenfield, on the other hand, takes a more optimistic view of the media's role in the political process in his work *Playing to Win.* Greenfield contends that the advent of a national media system has forced politicians to speak with the same voice in all regions of the country; allow greater public participation in the primary and electoral process, thereby limiting the influence of political power brokers; and permit candidates direct access to voters through televised advertisements. Overall, Greenfield feels that television's most important contribution to political campaigning relates to the homogenization of the process. Now, all members of the electorate can become actively involved in acquiring and filtering political information and acting upon it.

From a historical perspective, Edwin Diamond and Stephen Bates have written a highly readable analysis of political advertising entitled *The Spot: The Rise of Political Advertising on Television.* This work, which contains a wealth of examples, traces the origins of spot advertising from radio to television. It is an excellent blend of history, political strategy, creative process, and future implications. For those interested in the mass-mediated messages of political campaigns, this volume is required reading.

Theory and practice is the focus of *Political Campaign Communication* by Judith Trent and Robert Friedenberg. Part One of this volume reviews the role of communication in political campaigns, the functional stages of effective communication strategies, and the channels employed in the process. Part Two emphasizes the application process, including such elements as public speaking, debates, the organization of campaign communication systems, and the interpersonal context of political communication. This volume is well researched, thoroughly referenced, and very readable.

VOTING AND THE MEDIA

Starting points for understanding how the media influence the presidential campaign process are *The People's Choice,* by Paul Lazarsfeld, Bernard Berelson, and Hazel Gaudet, and *Voting,* by by Bernard Berelson, Paul Lazarsfeld, and William McPhee. *The People's Choice* originally appeared in 1944 and is now in its third edition. It traces the background characteristics of the electorate, analyzes the people who change their minds during the campaign, and concludes with a discussion of the sources of such influences. This book lays an important foundation for the understanding of the communication processes that influence voter behaviors. *Voting* attempts to explain how people come to vote as they do. It deals with such matters as voter perception of politics, how personal influence affects preference, the role of the mass media, and the nature of the issues in the campaign and how people react to them.

Perhaps one of the most controversial issues to arise in the national election process in many years is the televised election projection. The competitive nature of network television has fostered an attitude of "Let's be first to call the winner." Of course the impact of this approach has severely limited the participation of voters in the western regions of the United States. In 1980, NBC announced Ronald Reagan the winner at 8:15 p.m. Eastern Standard Time, almost four hours before the polls closed in California. The debate over this kind of activity has been strong and furious, with many calling for the outlawing of projections altogether. A complete analysis with suggestions for policy on this matter has been posited by Percy Tannenbaum and Leslie Kostrich in their work *Turned-On TV/Turned-Off Voters.* This work reviews the problem and the issues surrounding it, assesses the evidence, explores approaches to evaluation, and offers alternatives to both early return influences and exit polling influences.

THE PRESIDENTIAL RACE

An excellent introduction to the role that the mass media play in the presidential election process can be found in Thomas Patterson's

The Mass Media Election: How Americans Choose Their President. Patterson begins this book with a discussion of the origins of media campaigns, a review of the election news content, and an analysis of press coverage of such elements as issues and candidates. His work continues with a multichapter discussion of the audience and an assessment of the impact that the media have on presidential campaigns. This volume is one of the most comprehensive works available on the topic and should be included in every collection on the topic.

Patterson has long been recognized as one of the leading scholars in the field of political communication. Working with Robert McClure, he set out to study the 1972 presidential campaign by asking two basic questions: How manipulative is political television? How informative is political television? In the *Unseeing Eye,* the authors review and investigate the role television plays in building a candidate's public image, how television works to educate the electorate on the critical issues and events, and how much influence it has on the way people vote. Their findings indicate that individual voters are still very much in control of their votes and that television has little or no influence on voter choice.

David Weaver, et al., in *Media Agenda-Setting in a Presidential Election,* set out to look at political learning during an entire presidential election year. The first part of the book provides an introduction and theoretical overview to the idea of media agenda-setting. The major findings of many earlier studies are reviewed, and the chief issues and developments in agenda-setting research are discussed. The second section of the book concentrates on the role of television and newspapers in setting interest, issue, and image agendas throughout the election year. All in all, this detailed work offers a wealth of valuable information on the agenda-setting function of the media.

The Selling of the President, 1968, by Joe McGinniss, traces the techniques used in the Nixon campaign to create an image that would sell Richard Nixon to the American public. The concept of selling images rather than issues is said to have been born in this election. *Blue Smoke and Mirrors* is a comprehensive analysis of the Reagan-Carter election campaign of 1980. The authors, Jack Germond and Jules Witcover, trace the events in and around the Reagan-Carter campaigns in an effort to explain how Reagan won and why Carter lost. Germond and Witcover demonstrate how the pressures of real events—hostages, bad economic conditions, and so on—prevented the usual political imagery from taking hold. This work offers fascinating reading to the student of political campaigns and contemporary history.

There are a good number of excellent works on the presidential campaign of 1980. Michael Robinson and Margaret Sheehan's *Over the Wire and on TV* investigates the differences between print and broadcast coverage of the 1980 campaign. The two organizations that they studied were CBS and UPI, finding that broadcasting was not more superficial than print, that there was almost equal access to media by both major parties, and that both organizations "strictly avoided subjective assessments of the candidates and their positions on the issues." In *Television Coverage of the 1980 Presidential Election,* editor William Adams has assembled an excellent blend of scholars, critics, politicians, and insiders who provide an intriguing and diversified analysis of the election. This work looks at polling, conventions, debates, and media coverage and provides many useful insights for future research projects.

Newton Minow, John Bartlow, and Lee Mitchell have assembled an invaluable analysis of presidential uses of television in *Presidential Television.* While not solely concerned with campaigns for the job, Minow and his team provide clear, detailed, and highly readable accounts of how and why presidents used television. This work covers presidents Eisenhower, Kennedy, Johnson, and Nixon and is well referenced with an extensive appendix detailing Nixon's specific uses of the medium. Of similar interest is William Spragens's *The Presidency and the Mass Media in the Age of Television.* As a former reporter, this author provides a historical analysis of the relationship between presidents and the White House press corps dating from 1945.

TELEVISED DEBATES

Austin Ranney has assembled a collection of critical essays on the need for and value of presidential debates in *The Past and Future of Presidential Debates.* A major issue, whether or not televised debates should be mandated for major party candidates, is addressed. The definitive work on the 1976 Ford-Carter debates is *The Great Debates: Carter vs. Ford,* edited by Sidney Kraus. This work is a comprehensive chronicle that traces the events and actions that brought about the debates. Its 26 critical essays examine the ways in which the electorate used the debates and assesses their impact on voting decisions and the campaigns in general. In addition, the verbatim transcripts of the four debates make this an indispensable historical record. Following in the tradition of Kraus's 1962 version of the *Great Debates,* which chronicled the Nixon-Kennedy debates, this book will also go down as a landmark contribution to the literature of television and politics.

The Twentieth Century Fund Task Force on Televised Presidential Debates has prepared an insightful report which discusses the role, function, and worth of televised presidential debates in a work entitled *With the Nation Watching.* The task force, which was comprised of prominent individuals in broadcasting, journalism, and public affairs, concluded that debates are an important source of information for the voting public and that they should become an essential component of all presidential elections. The task force commented that presidential candidates have an obligation to participate in these debates. Also included in this report is a background paper by Lee Mitchell which discusses the historical development of presidential debates; the impact that television has had upon them; and how such elements as candidate image, voter participation, and debate sponsorship have been affected by the televising of the event.

Political analyst and critic Jeff Greenfield, in dispensing advice to political hopefuls in his work *Playing to Win* holds to one overriding, fundamental fact: "Television has changed our political life less radically than you have been told" (p. 152). He contends that television's influence in politics is more mythical than real, yet deserving of respect and understanding; most of all, it should be faced without fear. But where do we go from here? Do we know enough at this point to predict the future? Will Jane and John Citizen continue to accept what Dan Rather, Peter Jennings, or Tom Brokaw show and tell them? Or will they eventually become totally frustrated with not being able to talk back to the images on their screens, leaving analysts and politicians alike to face up to what may become unmanageable public opinion? If Marshall McLuhan is right, it may be far too early to foresee just exactly how the electronic revolution will affect the way we perceive the experience and with what consequences.

BIBLIOGRAPHY

Adams, William C., ed. *Television Coverage of the 1980 Presidential Campaign.* Norwood, NJ: Ablex, 1983.

Benjamin, Gerald, ed. *The Communications Revolution in Politics.* New York: Academy of Political Science, 1982.

Berelson, Bernard; Lazarsfeld, Paul F.; and McPhee, William N. *Voting: A Study of Opinion Formation in a Presidential Campaign.* Chicago: University of Chicago Press, 1954.

Chaffee, Steven H., ed. *Political Communication: Issues and Strategies for Research.* Beverly Hills, CA: Sage, 1975.

Diamond, Edwin, and Bates, Stephan. *The Spot: The Rise of Political Advertising on Television.* Cambridge, MA: MIT Press, 1984.

Germond, Jack W., and Witcover, Jules. *Blue Smoke and Mirrors: How Reagan Won and Why Carter Lost the Election of 1980.* New York: Viking, 1981.

Graber, Doris. *Mass Media and American Politics.* Washington, DC: Congressional Quarterly, Inc., 1980.

Greenfield, Jeff. *Playing to Win: An Insider's Guide to Politics.* New York: Simon & Schuster, 1980.

Kraus, Sidney, ed. *The Great Debates: Background, Perspective, Effects.* Bloomington, IN: Indiana University Press, 1962.

———. *The Great Debates: Carter vs. Ford, 1976.* Bloomington, IN: Indiana University Press, 1979.

Kraus, Sidney, and Davis, Dennis. *The Effects of Mass Communication on Political Behavior.* University Park, PA: Pennsylvania State University Press, 1976.

Lazarsfeld, Paul F.; Berelson, Bernard; and Gaudet, Hazel. *The People's Choice: How the Voter Makes Up His Mind in a Presidential Campaign.* 3d ed. New York: Columbia University Press, 1968.

MacKuen, Michael B., and Coombs, Steven L. *More than News: Media Power in Public Affairs.* Beverly Hills, CA: Sage, 1981.

McGinniss, Joe. *The Selling of the President, 1968.* New York: Trident Press, 1969.

Meadow, Robert G. *Politics as Communication.* Norwood, NJ: Ablex, 1980.

Mickelson, Sig. *The Electric Mirror: Politics in an Age of Television.* New York: Dodd, Mead, 1972.

Minow, Newton; Bartlow, John; and Mitchell, Lee M. *Presidential Television.* New York: Basic Books, 1973.

Nimmo, Dan, and Combs, James. *Mediated Political Realities.* New York: Longman, 1983.

Paletz, David L., and Entman, Robert M. *Media, Power, Politics.* New York: Macmillan, 1981.

Patterson, Thomas. *The Mass Media Election: How Americans Choose Their President.* New York: Praeger, 1980.

Patterson, Thomas, and McClure, Robert. *The Unseeing Eye: The Myth of Television Power in National Elections.* New York: Putnam, 1976.

Ranney, Austin. *Channels of Power: The Impact of Television on American Politics.* New York: Basic Books, 1983.

Ranney, Austin, ed. *The Past and Future of Presidential Debates.* Washington, DC: American Enterprise Institute for Public Policy Research, 1979.

Robinson, Michael J., and Sheehan, Margaret. *Over the Wire and on TV: CBS and UPI in Campaign '80.* New York: Russell Sage Foundation, 1983.

Saldich, Anne Rawley. *Electronic Democracy: Television's Impact on the American Political Process.* New York: Praeger, 1979.

Spragens, William C. *The Presidency and Mass Media in the Age of Television.* Washington, DC: University Press of America, 1978.

Tannenbaum, Percy H., and Kostrich, Leslie J. *Turned-On TV/Turned-Off Voters: Policy Options for Election Projections.* Beverly Hills, CA: Sage, 1983.

Trent, Judith S., and Friedenberg, Robert. *Political Campaign Communication: Principles and Practices.* New York: Praeger, 1983.

Tunstall, Jeremy, and Walker, David. *Media Made in California: Hollywood, Politics, and the News.* New York: Oxford University Press, 1981.

Twentieth Century Fund. *With the Nation Watching: Report of the Twentieth Century Fund Task Force on Televised Presidential Debates.* New York: Lexington Books, 1979.

Weaver, David H., et al., eds. *Media Agenda-Setting in a Presidential Election: Issues, Images, and Interest.* New York: Praeger, 1981.

Part III
Directions

Introduction

Several recent publications have attempted to define the contemporary American television environment and to assess the dimension of its influence. These documents point out that TV's persuasiveness and its cumulative saturation of the American culture under conditions that neither demand nor extract the viewers' full attention have produced a viewership that shares uniformly in the same appalling lack of critical scrutiny. Despite this, the claim is made that the "on" switch of our TV sets tunes us in to the collective consciousness of our country and that sooner or later whatever our society considers important—whether it is standards of morality, government activity, or crime and punishment—will show up in some form on our TV screens.

Furthermore, the stories illustrating television's power to heighten viewer passions and frustrations are legion. The first known case of videocide (but certainly not the last) was reported in a brief news item in 1953. It seems that an otherwise "laid-back," law-abiding citizen became so infuriated with the talking images on his screen, whom he could neither answer nor ignore, that he picked up his gun and shot his set full of holes! Now, nearly 30 years later, little of the sound and fury over television's negative effects has abated and the polemics about TV corrupting the moral fiber of our society are being heard even more loudly throughout the country. Many of television's self-proclaimed critics would solve the problem they perceive of television's antisocial effects by having us not only unplug our sets but perhaps also chop them up for firewood. But such an approach, even if spearheaded by millions of proponents, could not possibly work, for the tens of millions who have come to depend upon television for so much could hardly be persuaded to give it up.

Few will dispute the statement that television is "The Force" to be reckoned with today. It is our frame of reference for viewing the various dimensions of our society, for evaluating the quality of our culture, and for setting the agenda of our priorities. It has an impact upon our values and beliefs and our sociopsychological and aesthetic perception. This "force" is so powerful and pervasive that we tend to regard it as something that has been around for a long, long time, even though when measured in the context of the lifespan of all communication throughout the ages, television has been with us for only a brief moment. Yet, because of television's pervasiveness and potency, there must be a concern for its patterns of growth and development—to ensure that its future directions will be distinguished by careful thought and integrity. It is our view that the directions that television will take in the future lie not only, though importantly, in the hands of the television industry, professional critics, and the field's seminal thinkers, but also with all the people—nonviewers as well as viewers—who care about the quality of life.

Chapter 8
The Television Industry

OVERVIEW

The television industry is a potent economic force, both as a business and marketing tool. As an economic force of this magnitude, it carries with it many benefits as well as drawbacks. To begin with, the confusing arrangement whereby the viewer is sold to the advertiser, in bundles of a thousand homes, goes counter to the impression that most people have about advertisers simply buying "airtime." The more cynical student of broadcasting might conclude that television programs are little more than spacers that separate the commercials, but for the most part, people do accept the necessity of such an arrangement. The optimistic student of the medium, on the other hand, might ask: "If things are so bad, then how would one explain the fact that the broadcasting industry in the U.S. is the largest, most successful, and most demanded program supplier in the world?" Of course, we all know that quantity does not necessarily correlate with quality and that TV program survival via popularity polls is supposed to be the best means for giving the public what it wants. On the other hand, there are those who feel that because of this, television rarely gives us what we need. The controversy goes on and on.

Aside from participating in the philosophical discussions of the medium, television must also do daily battle in its own volatile environment. It competes against itself—network against network, station against station, and program supplier against program supplier. It competes in a regulatory arena consisting of government agencies, politicians, lobbyists, and numerous pressure groups. It competes with the new technologies—cable, satellites, home video recorders and games, and very soon, new low-power broadcast stations and direct-broadcast satellites. Without any doubt, in a system such as this, the stakes are likely to be astronomical, and it would not be unusual for the interests of the public to conflict with—and lose to—other financial or personal interests. On the other hand, the television system in the U.S. is still the most diverse and bountiful of any in the world.

This chapter focuses on the literature about television as an industry, giving special attention to its regulation and programming; the new technologies that surround it; and some analysis from both insiders and outsiders about how it became what it is, why it remains so, and what it will take to change it.

CONTROL AND INFLUENCE

A theme that flows through many critical works on the medium deals with the oligopolistic structure of the industry. With three networks controlling the greatest proportion of programming and access to the airwaves, little room remains for diversity and competition in the free marketplace. These issues and many more are presented in *Network Television and the Public Interest,* edited by Michael Botein and David Rice, as well as in *The Networks* by A. Frank Reel. Botein and Rice present 22 papers from a conference held at the New York Law School in 1978 where issues on network programming, distribution, regulation, and access were discussed. In Reel's work, the growth of network power is traced; then the author posits various views as to how such a structure has "robbed television of its potential."

Many works tend to focus on the individuals who wield power in the television industry. Here the concern is that a limited few make decisions for the many on the shape and direction of television. The man most often written about in terms of this theme is William S. Paley, board chair of CBS. A variety of fascinating anecdotes and solid analysis can be found in *The Powers that Be,* by David Halberstam, *Due to Circumstances beyond Our Control,* by Fred Friendly, and *See No Evil,* by Geoffrey Cowan. Each of these talented writers offers personal insights into the complex power relationships that exist in the corporation boardrooms of America's media giants. Perhaps the darkest example of how this concentration of power in the hands of a few can destroy the freedom and rights of the many can be found in Karen Sue Foley's *The Political Blacklist in the Broadcast Industry.* This superbly researched volume presents a historical analysis of the broadcast industry's participation in the hunt for communists in the entertainment business. Foley indicates that, because of the widespread anticommunist atmosphere, the broadcast industry's fear of controversy, and industry preoccupation with "image," a handful of people pressured employers into screening and blacklisting employees.

An excellent volume that explores at length the impact and influence of media conglomerates is Ben Bagdikian's *The Media Monopoly.* This work is heavily referenced and contains a wealth of statistical information, but none of this material limits its readability. Bagdikian has blended the hard facts with interesting anecdotes, solid analysis, and fascinating insights into the industry. This book certainly deserves the attention of scholars, researchers, and students whose interests focus on the media industry and its social and economic roles.

Two additional volumes, while very different from each other, provide unique and important overviews to their respective areas of the industry. Tony Schwartz, in *Media: The Second God,* discusses at length his interpretation of, and role in, the creation of messages for television. Schwartz, perhaps best known as the creator of Lyndon Johnson's now famous political spot entitled "Daisy," which contrasted an atomic explosion with a young girl picking flowers, talks of how he develops advertisements that are effective and his philosophy behind their creation. This work is not just a "how to" kind of narrative, but more appropriately a "why it works" kind of discussion. *Small Voices and Great Trumpets,* edited by Bernard Rubin, is a collection of critical essays and research papers on minorities and the media. This volume takes a diverse view of the topic, dealing with the issue of minorities in terms of the images presented in the media, the legal implications of representation and access, and the role of advocacy as a method to influence the system.

REGULATION AND POLICY

The regulation of the broadcast industry is a continuing struggle among government, industry, and a multitude of special interest groups. How much regulation is needed to ensure responsible operation by the various licensees? What should be regulated? Who should decide? How do people know whether or not they are complying with the regulations? These questions and issues arise each year and countless interest groups input their specific points of view on such elements as licensing, the fairness doctrine, program content, program diversity, advertising policy, and fair use.

Two works that offer excellent overviews of regulation are *Law of Mass Communications,* by Harold Nelson and Dwight Teeter, and *Fact and Fancy in TV Regulation,* by Harvey Levin. *Law of Mass Communications* is a fundamental work that tracks the growth and development of this area of U.S. law and the implications for the communications industry. Dividing their book into two major areas, the authors begin by discussing the multifaceted aspects of libel, copyright, privacy, free press-fair trial, and obscenity. The second area deals with public interest in communications law. Access rights, advertising regulation, antitrust laws, and licensing are given extensive analysis. *Fact and Fancy in TV Regulation* looks at this issue from an economic point of view. Levin combines case studies with extensive data from the FCC in his analysis of the regulation process.

The fairness doctrine is one of the most controversial regulations in broadcasting today. The seemingly simple requirement that broadcasters air programs on important, controversial issues in a fair way becomes extremely complex when one attempts to determine what is fair and who should make that decision. Two works offer excellent analysis of the regulation. *The Fairness Doctrine and the Media,* written by Steven Simmons, an expert on communications and constitutional law, offers an invaluable guide to the development of the regulation as well as practical information on how to comply with it. The extensive citations and a separate case and document index, in addition to the general subject index, make this work a valuable asset to researchers and broadcasters alike. Fred Friendly's *The Good Guys, the Bad Guys, and the First Amendment* looks at the fairness doctrine as an issue of free speech versus fairness in broadcasting.

The ways in which broadcasters fulfill their obligation to serve the public interest is explored from two different perspectives. The first work, by Donald Guimary, *Citizen's Groups and Broadcasting* surveys citizen involvement in commercial broadcasting in an effort to discover how these groups formed and evolved, what their impact has been on the industry, and what the reaction of commercial and public broadcasters has been to their participation. William Rivers, Wilbur Schramm, and Clifford Christians looked at the ethical dimensions of serving the public interest in *Responsibility in Mass Communication.* The third edition of this seminal work addresses the concept of responsibility in mass communication from three different perspectives, in addition to discussing the nature of regulation and censorship in the media. It also proposes various methods through which the mass media can provide fair and truthful information along with a diversity of entertainment.

The regulation process has never been a simple matter of making and following the rules, as is pointed out in two works that look at the politics and compromises that go on in the Federal Communications Commission. Erwin Krasnow, Lawrence Longley, and Herbert Terry provide an excellent introduction to the regulatory process in *The Poli-*

tics of Broadcast Regulation. The greater part of the book consists of five case studies that exemplify the controversial and political nature of broadcast regulation. In another work, Barry Cole and Mel Oettinger provide a fascinating inside look at the regulation process in *Reluctant Regulators.* This eminently readable book combines numerous examples with insightful analysis of all aspects of the work of the Federal Communications Commission.

The process through which one obtains and retains a broadcasting license is discussed in Terry Ellmore's *Broadcasting Law and Regulation.* Topics covered include a history of broadcast regulation, the FCC, allocation, assignment, licensing, technical and program regulations, cable television, the future of broadcasting law, and legal research. An exploration of two points of view with regard to regulation can be found in John Bittner's *Broadcast Law and Regulation.* In an effort to provide balance between the larger policy issues that face broadcasters and their day-to-day implementation of those policies, Bittner looks at the overall regulatory environment in which each licensee must operate. William Francois, in his work *Mass Media Law and Regulation,* discusses the regulatory process from a somewhat broader perspective, which includes such elements as First Amendment considerations, libel, prior restraint, freedom of information, subpoena power and reporter privilege, and antitrust laws and media ownership concentration.

For those researchers interested in specific cases that relate to broadcast regulation, Marvin Bensman, in *Broadcast Regulation: Selected Cases and Decisions,* summarizes 564 FCC and judicial court cases, each with full legal citations. The primary emphasis of these cases is on programming. Without a doubt, this volume is one of the most valuable primary resource works available in the area. In *Law and the Television of the 80's,* Norman Redlich and Gerald Crane have collected 11 original papers that were presented at a 1980 New York University Law School conference. Issues covered include two-way TV and privacy, cable franchises and local regulation, copyright and the newer technologies, media ownership, and the fate of public broadcasting.

Mass Media and the Supreme Court: The Legacy of the Warren Years is an edited collection assembled by Kenneth Devol. The focus of this volume is on the Supreme Court's media-related decisions, including items such as prior restraint, access, obscenity, censorship, libel, and media publicity of trials. Richard Lubinski, in his book *The First Amendment under Siege: The Politics of Broadcast Regulation,* articulates an interesting perspective with regard to free speech for broadcasters. Suggesting that broadcasters have not fought hard enough to gain independence from many of the speech-constraining regulations within which they operate, he discusses this thesis along with a number of other regulation-related concerns.

Broadcast Fairness, by Ford Rowan, is an excellent, detailed analysis of this important broadcasting rule. Rowan approaches this topic with a thorough review of the development, intent, and application of the rule; a case study in its use; an explication of its implementation; and a discussion of its risks and drawbacks. Michael Botein and David Rice's edited volume *Network Television in the Public Interest: A Preliminary Inquiry* presents a number of perspectives on the power in and around the broadcast industry and points out a number of essential policy issues that are currently being faced by the industry. Public input and sharing of the power are taking-off points for a number of the works in this volume.

PROGRAMMING

The process of programming for television has at different times been characterized as an art, a science, or a random gamble. The people who schedule the programming of America's airwaves have been variously described as 12-year-olds masquerading as adults, as geniuses who can predict the mood of the audience, or as villains who are getting very rich underestimating the taste of viewers.

Aside from how one might feel about the current state of television programming, the very process of programming is very important and too often overlooked—especially during those recurring discussions about the poor quality of television in which we all engage. Included here are a number of works that offer some excellent insights into the programming process. Gaye Tuchman's *The TV Establishment,* for example, is a collection of essays written from the critical as well as the practical perspectives, and it serves as a valuable overview of the process. Susan Eastman, Sydney Head, and Lewis Klein's *Broadcast Programming* offers a comprehensive look at the strategies and underlying principles of broadcast programming. The authors address programming for local and network operations and also analyze the role and function of specific program types. Included are sections on pay TV, super stations, and radio programming.

V. Jackson Smith provides a brief analysis of programming in *Programming for Radio and Television.* Building on a historical background, Smith looks at the nature of the audience, the elements of a successful program, and the methods of program evaluation. Charles Clift and Archie Greer's *Broadcast Programming: The Current Perspec-*

tive is a fascinating mix of articles from various broadcast trade journals, divided along such lines as ratings, schedules, program types, local programming, and regulation. This work, issued annually, can be regarded as a useful reference document for each television season or as a media course workbook or reader.

Window Dressing on the Set and *Window Dressing on the Set: An Update,* both reports prepared for the U.S. Commission on Civil Rights, provide an excellent account of how women and minorities are portrayed in television programming and how well the television industry is serving the public interest. These reports are replete with valuable quantitative data not easily obtained elsewhere as well as interesting analyses of programming trends beginning with the 1950s and continuing through the mid-1970s.

Two works that look at the organizational aspects of the media industry and its influence on programming are *Media Industries: The Production of News and Entertainment,* by Joseph Turow, and *Individuals in Mass Media Organizations,* by James Ettema and D. Charles Whitney. Turow focuses on the range of competition that exists among various media organizations and the nature of their cooperative production and distribution relationships, all with an eye toward answering two fundamental questions: "What maintains continuity and creates change in content and quality of these materials?" and "To what extent can members of the public influence or effect change?" Ettema and Whitney, as editors of *Individuals in Mass Media Organizations,* have collected a series of academic perspectives on the ways in which organizational constraints affect the creativity of individuals in media organizations. This work provides a broad view, with chapters dealing with music, book publishing, TV entertainment, and TV journalism, to name just a few.

Television Programming for News and Public Affairs, by Frank Wolf, provides a quantitative analysis of public affairs and news programming in the top 50 television markets in the U.S. This book is an excellent account of the nature and extent of this program genre and indicates the major influences that determine the frequency and quality of the broadcasts. As might be expected, the financial resources of each station play a significant role in this area. Approaching the programming perspective of television from a very different angle, Horace Newcomb and Robert Alley, in *The Producer's Medium,* share with their readers a number of fascinating conversations that they had with the "creators of American TV"—the producers. These revealing comments from well-known television producers are enhanced by Newcomb and Alley's extensive annotations. This glimpse into the minds and hearts of the industry professionals will serve as a valuable resource for all students of television.

One of the fastest growing and most controversial aspects of television programming is the religious broadcast. Jeffrey Hadden and Charles Swann, in *Prime Time Preachers,* explore the rising power of this program form and profile the many significant individuals who have influenced its growth. In addition, the authors analyze the new "electronic church" in terms of program styles, financial resources, and political involvement. The Moral Majority is given special attention as well.

Two works which effectively transcend the barriers between academia and popular interest are *Stay Tuned: An Inside Look at the Making of Prime Time Television,* by Richard Levinson and William Link, and *Up the Tube: Prime-Time TV and the Silverman Years,* by Sally Bedell. Both works are highly readable, thought-provoking accounts of the "behind-the-scenes" operations of the broadcast industry. The superb blending of personalities, business concerns, and creative conflict will present readers with an integrated perspective on how things go in, go on, and come out of the process.

PUBLIC BROADCASTING

Much too often, the television industry is thought of solely in terms of the commercial networks and their local affiliates, relegating the unique role played by public broadcasting in the U.S. to the minor leagues. An excellent starting point for those interested in the historical origins of educational and public broadcasting can be found in George Gibson's *Public Broadcasting.* Beginning with 1912, Gibson traces the role of the federal government in public broadcasting, detailing the many contributions of presidents, congresspersons, and various government agencies. Of similar appeal is Robert Blakely's *To Serve the Public Interest: Educational Broadcasting in the United States.* Blakely effectively recounts and interprets the growth and development of public broadcasting, beginning with its early days as ITV on through to its current status as a multifaceted public service. This work provides a good deal of insight into the individuals and groups who shaped public broadcasting, the interrelationships among public and commercial broadcasting efforts as well as the influence of government, philanthropic, and community agencies.

Perhaps the best known and most important documents on public broadcasting are the two Carnegie Commission reports, *Public Televi-*

sion: A Program for Action, issued in 1967, and *A Public Trust,* released in 1979. The 1967 Carnegie report was the driving force behind the congressional action that created the public broadcasting system as it exists today. The 1979 report evaluates the system and proposes changes that would diversify and strengthen public broadcasting.

The Future of Public Broadcasting, edited by Douglass Cater and Michael Nyham, is a volume of essays that address policy issues relevant to public broadcasting. The editors label the contributors as "middle range visionaries who are neither blue-sky dreamers nor day-to-day tacticians" (p. vii). The charge given each contributor was to identify existing problems in the public broadcasting system, explore a range of possible solutions, and conclude with proposals for the future direction of public broadcasting in the United States.

NEW TECHNOLOGIES

The incredibly rapid growth of new technologies in the communications industry has prompted some to predict the end of television networks and the beginning of a new era of quality programs. Neither has happened so far, but the development of cable television systems and home video recorders and the promise of video discs for every possible use have awakened many to the potential for diversified programming sources that will serve the varied interests of many publics, not just the mass audience. An outstanding work edited by Glen Robinson, *Communications for Tomorrow,* addresses the policy implications of the new communications technology in society. The regulation and application of the new electronic media are discussed along with the role of government in the policymaking process.

Stuart De Luca's *Television's Transformation* and Vincent Mosco's *Broadcasting in the United States* look at the future of television from the perspective of how new technologies will change it and how regulation and political maneuvering will limit it. Although De Luca's book provides the reader with technical background on the development of television, it remains very useful and readable even for the novice. This background sets the stage for a chapter-by-chapter discussion of new technologies such as cable, home video, and satellites. Mosco presents a somewhat more historical view of the development of new technologies. His analysis places these technologies within the economic and social as well as the regulatory environments. These two works combine to offer a comprehensive picture from many perspectives. A slightly less optimistic view is presented by John Wicklein in *Electronic Night-*

mare. Although he acknowledges the potential benefits deriving from the interconnectedness of our communication systems, Wicklein feels we must act expeditiously to minimize the risks that threaten our own privacy and pose a danger for censorship and unchecked control of information by governments or large conglomerates.

Paula Dranov, Louise Moore, and Adrienne Hickey explore the uses of television in business, education, medicine, and government in their work *Video in the 80's.* This volume explores the nonbroadcast uses of television. Using data collected from various agencies, the authors provide specific case studies and practical suggestions as to how the various new technologies can be employed in numerous situations. Of similar importance, Efrem Sigel, Mark Schubin, and Paul Merrill's *Video Discs* looks at the development, application, and future of this infant industry. Herbert Howard and S.L. Carroll's *Subscription Television: History, Current Status, and Economic Projections* takes a close look at a specific technological development. This comprehensive report, as the subtitle suggests, traces history, state of the art, and economic future of both over-the-air and cable subscription television services. Sheila Mahoney, Nick DeMartino, and Robert Stengel discuss the potential of new technologies to assist public television's quest for financial stability in *Keeping PACE with the New Television.* The authors propose the development of a national, nonprofit, pay cable channel programmed by public television, with income from it used to support public television broadcast channels.

Because video technology has made copying of television programs possible, the argument over "fair use" of copyrighted media materials has become one of the most complex issues facing the broadcast industry today. *Fair Use and Free Inquiry,* edited by John Lawrence and Bernard Timberg, explores this controversy in terms of its impact on the teacher, scholar, and researcher. The 24 essays in this book offer a comprehensive analysis of the copyright law as it relates to various media, beginning with an overview of the origins of fair use and copyright, followed by numerous perspectives on how the law affects the users and producers of media, and concluding with a number of proposals that attempt to strike a compromise among the many concerned parties.

An area of growing concern with regard to the growth and adoption of new communications technologies is their impact on the social, economic, and political aspects of our society. Four works address these issues from varying perspectives. Wilson Dizard, in *The Coming Information Age,* blends three crucial elements—technology, economics, and politics—in his probing analysis of the information age. Dizard provides extensive discussion of such elements as communication networks, computer-based information systems, the economic and political realities of new technologies, perspectives on information exporting, and the United States' future as influenced by these forces. Frederick Williams reviews the historical role of mass communication and discusses how new technologies have developed within a framework of social and economic forces in *The Communications Revolution.* Williams sees much of what is happening in communications today as very similar to other social revolutions—ranking it among the likes of the industrial and the agricultural revolutions. He is convinced that future historians will see this era as "another great transition in the evolution of our civilization" (p. 245). Projecting the future of communications is the focus of a volume which emerged from a 1981 symposium jointly sponsored by the University of Virginia's Colgate Darden Graduate School of Business Administration and the Annenberg Schools of Communication. *Communications in the Twenty-First Century,* edited by Robert Haigh, George Gerbner, and Richard Byrne, consists of 20 original papers from a variety of perspectives, exploring such topics as interactive communications, free-flow of information, numerous "media outlooks," and public policy issues as they relate to social, managerial, and technical dimensions of communication in the twenty-first century. The final work in this group deals specifically with the policy aspects of new communications technology. John Howkins, working from a British perspective in his book *New Technologies, New Policies?,* analyzes the dimensions of policy across the entire spectrum of concerns—technical, legal, financial, social, and political. His discussion covers both the philosophical and the practical aspects of creating and implementing policy in this area.

Finding that the growth of new technologies is less a concern than the public policy that surrounds it, Ithiel de Sola Pool, in *Technologies of Freedom,* sees the many diverse media converging into one medium—the electronic. His major concern over this homogenization of communication systems is with the regulatory environment that currently surrounds the broadcast technology and, by default, will surround previously unregulated communication forms such as newspapers—once they become part of teletext systems. Pool explores the implications of these policies with regard to First Amendment guarantees, the fairness doctrine, and the individual's right of public access to the media.

While cable communications is not that "new" of a technology when compared to DBS and Low Power TV, it does remain one of the most potentially influential technologies on the scene today. An excellent overview of this "potential" can be found in Thomas Baldwin and D. Steven McVoy's *Cable Communications.* This volume covers the range of services possible on cable systems, the operational/managerial aspects, the public policy concerns, and also the role of changing technology on the future of cable. Looking at cable from a programming angle, Kirsten Beck, in her work *Cultivating the Wasteland,* provides a comprehensive guide to the existing and future program possibilities for cable. Beck explores programming for cable from many sides—from local access to negotiating with major program producers. This work will serve as a useful resource for the practitioner and scholar alike.

ECONOMICS

Commentary on the structure and direction of the television industry is broad based and plentiful. If one had to select a single theme that appears most often in the works analyzing the television industry, it would have to be the recurring criticism over the commercial nature of the medium. *Inside the TV Business,* edited and written by Paul Klein and nine other industry insiders, openly and sometimes regretfully admits to the bottom-line reality of the television business. Each of the eight essays in this volume addresses the special concerns of one aspect of the industry—Klein looks at programming, Don Ohlmeyer at sports, Richard Wald at news, and so on. The valuable insights the authors offer about their respective specialties are at times overshadowed by the occasional frustration they express about the structure of the industry that they too must live under.

However, in terms of criticism, it appears that the informed outsider is far less tolerant of the frustrating structure than the insiders. Les Brown, in *Television: The Business behind the Box,* and Erik Barnouw, in *The Sponsor,* look critically at the financial aspect of television. The combination of quality writing and astute observation makes these books required reading for the student of television. Kent Anderson underscores the points made by Brown and Barnouw in *Television Fraud,* which traces the history and consequences of the quiz show scandals that rocked the television industry in the mid-1950s. The advertiser-encouraged fixing of the quiz shows for the sake of higher ratings shocked audiences across the country and resulted in congressional hearings and new industry guidelines.

John Wright, in *The Commercial Connection,* has assembled a collection of readings that grapple with the much debated role advertising has played, still plays, and will continue to play in American mass media. This book covers the background and foreground of the advertising/media relationship; explores the tie that binds advertising and media together—the audience; confronts the major issues concerning the advertising/media role; and finally takes a behind-the-scenes look at the creative side of advertising. As an annual volume, the *Advertising Age Yearbook* serves as an excellent resource on the year-to-year happenings on the financial and marketing side of the television industry. This work is put together primarily from articles that appeared in the highly respected industry trade journal *Advertising Age* and will make a valuable addition to most collections.

In summary, the fierce competition for supremacy among the giant networks; the never-ending struggle in the political arena for regulation and deregulation; the race to be first to develop and harness new technologies; and the ever-increasing pressure to confront television's detractors are but a few of the complexities that confound our understanding of television as an industry.

BIBLIOGRAPHY

Advertising Age Yearbook, 1982. Chicago: Crain Books, 1982.

Anderson, Kent. *Television Fraud: The History and Implications of the Quiz Show Scandals.* Westport, CT: Greenwood, 1978.

Bagdikian, Ben H. *The Media Monopoly.* Boston: Beacon Press, 1983.

Baldwin, Thomas F., and McVoy, D. Steven. *Cable Communication.* Englewood Cliffs, NJ: Prentice-Hall, 1983.

Barnouw, Erik. *The Sponsor: Notes on a Modern Potentate.* New York: Oxford University Press, 1978.

Beck, Kirsten. *Cultivating the Wasteland: Can Cable Put the Vision Back in TV?* New York: American Council for the Arts, 1983.

Bedell, Sally. *Up the Tube: Prime-Time TV and the Silverman Years.* New York: Viking, 1981.

Bensman, Marvin R. *Broadcast Regulation: Selected Cases and Decisions.* Lanham, MD: University Press of America, 1983.

Bittner, John R. *Broadcast Law and Regulation.* Englewood Cliffs, NJ: Prentice-Hall, 1982.

Blakely, Robert J. *To Serve the Public Interest: Educational Broadcasting in the United States.* Syracuse, NY: Syracuse University Press, 1979.

Botein, Michael, and Rice, David M., eds. *Network Television and the Public Interest: A Primary Inquiry.* Lexington, MA: D.C. Heath, 1980.

Brown, Les. *Television: The Business behind the Box.* New York: Harcourt, Brace, Jovanovich, 1971.

Carnegie Commission on Educational Television. *Public Television: A Program for Action.* New York: Harper & Row, 1967.

Carnegie Commission on the Future of Public Broadcasting. *A Public Trust: The Report of the Carnegie Commission on the Future of Public Broadcasting.* New York: Bantam Books, 1979.

Cater, Douglass, and Nyhan, Michael J., eds. *The Future of Public Broadcasting.* New York: Praeger, 1976.

Clift, Charles, and Greer, Archie, eds. *Broadcast Programming: The Current Perspective.* Washington, DC: University Press of America, 1976–.

Cole, Barry G., and Oettinger, Mel. *Reluctant Regulators: The FCC and the Broadcast Audience.* Rev. ed. Reading, MA: Addison-Wesley, 1978.

Cowan, Geoffrey. *See No Evil: The Backstage Battle over Sex and Violence on Television.* New York: Simon & Schuster, 1979.

De Luca, Stuart M. *Television's Transformation: The Next 25 Years.* New York: A. S. Barnes, 1980.

Devol, Kenneth S., ed. *Mass Media and the Supreme Court: The Legacy of the Warren Years.* 3d ed. New York: Hastings House, 1982.

Dizard, Wilson P., Jr. *The Coming Information Age: An Overview of Technology, Economics, and Politics.* New York: Longman, 1982.

Dranov, Paula; Moore, Louise; and Hickey, Adrienne. *Video in the 80's: Emerging Uses for Television in Business, Education, Medicine, and Government.* White Plains, NY: Knowledge Industry, 1980.

Eastman, Susan Tyler; Head, Sydney W.; and Klein, Lewis. *Broadcast Programming: Strategies for Winning Television and Radio Audiences.* Belmont, CA: Wadsworth, 1981.

Ellmore, R. Terry. *Broadcasting Law and Regulation.* Blue Ridge, PA: Tab Books, 1982.

Ettema, James S., and Whitney, D. Charles *Individuals in Mass Media Organizations: Creativity and Constraint.* Beverly Hills, CA: Sage, 1982.

Foley, Karen Sue. *The Political Blacklist in the Broadcast Industry: The Decade of the 1950's.* New York: Arno, 1979.

Francois, William E. *Mass Media Law and Regulation.* Columbus, OH: Grid Publications, 1982.

Friendly, Fred W. *Due to Circumstances beyond Our Control.* New York: Random House, 1967.

———. *The Good Guys, the Bad Guys, and the First Amendment: Free Speech vs. Fairness in Broadcasting.* New York: Random House, 1976.

Gibson, George. *Public Broadcasting: The Role of the Federal Government, 1912–1976.* New York: Praeger, 1977.

Guimary, Donald L. *Citizen's Groups and Broadcasting.* New York: Praeger, 1975.

Hadden, Jeffrey, and Swann, Charles E. *Prime Time Preachers: The Rising Power of Televangelism.* Reading, MA: Addison-Wesley, 1981.

Haigh, Robert W.; Gerbner, George; and Byrne, Richard B. *Communications in the Twenty-First Century.* New York: Wiley-Interscience, 1981.

Halberstam, David. *The Powers that Be.* New York: Knopf, 1979.

Howard, Herbert H., and Carroll, S.L. *Subscription Television: History, Current Status, and Economic Projections.* Knoxville, TN: University of Tennessee Press, 1980.

Howkins, John. *New Technologies, New Policies? A Report for the Broadcasting Research Unit.* New York: Zoetrope, 1983.

Klein, Paul, et al. *Inside the TV Business.* New York: Sterling, 1979.

Krasnow, Erwin G.; Longley, Lawrence D.; and Terry, Herbert. *The Politics of Broadcast Regulation.* 3d ed. New York: St Martin's Press, 1982.

Lawrence, John Shelton, and Timberg, Bernard, eds. *Fair Use and Free Inquiry: Copyright Law and the New Media.* Norwood, NJ: Ablex, 1980.

Levin, Harvey J. *Fact and Fancy in TV Regulation: An Economic Study of Policy Alternatives.* Beverly Hills, CA: Sage, 1980.

Levinson, Richard, and Link, William. *Stay Tuned: An Inside Look at the Making of Prime Time Television.* New York: St. Martin's Press, 1981.

Lubonski, Richard E. *The First Amendment under Siege: The Politics of Broadcast Regulation.* Westport, CT: Greenwood, 1981.

Mahoney, Sheila; DeMartino, Nick; and Stengel, Robert. *Keeping PACE with the New Television: Public Television and Changing Technology.* New York: Carnegie, 1980.

Mosco, Vincent. *Broadcasting in the United States: Innovative Challenge and Organizational Control.* Norwood, NJ: Ablex, 1979.

Nelson, Harold L., and Teeter, Dwight L. *Law of Mass Communications: Freedom and Control of Print and Broadcast Media.* 3d ed. Mineola, NY: Foundation Press, 1978.

Newcomb, Horace, and Alley, Robert S., eds. *The Producer's Medium: Conversations with Creators of American TV.* New York: Oxford University Press, 1983.

Pool, Ithiel de Sola. *Technologies of Freedom.* Cambridge, MA: Harvard University Press, 1983.

Redlich, Norman, and Crane, Gerald, eds. *Law and the Television of the 80's.* New York: NYU School of Law, 1983.

Reel, A. Frank. *The Networks: How They Stole the Show.* New York: Scribner, 1979.

Rivers, William L.; Schramm, Wilbur; and Christians, Clifford. *Responsibility in Mass Communication.* 3d ed. New York: Harper & Row, 1980.

Robinson, Glen O., ed. *Communications for Tomorrow: Policy Perspectives for the 1980's.* New York: Praeger, 1978.

Rowan, Ford. *Broadcast Fairness.* New York: Longman, 1984.

Rubin, Bernard, ed. *Small Voices and Great Trumpets: Minorities and the Media.* New York: Praeger, 1980.

Schwartz, Tony. *Media: The Second God.* New York: Random House, 1982.

Sigel, Efrem; Schubin, Mark; and Merrill, Paul. *Video Discs: The Technology, the Applications and the Future.* White Plains, NY: Knowledge Industry, 1980.

Simmons, Steven J. *The Fairness Doctrine and the Media.* Berkeley, CA: University of California Press, 1978.

Smith, V. Jackson. *Programming for Radio and TV.* Rev. ed Washington, DC: University Press of America, 1983.

Tuchman, Gaye. *The TV Establishment: Programming for Power and Profit.* Englewood Cliffs, NJ: Prentice-Hall, 1974.

Turow, Joseph. *Media Industries: The Production of News and Entertainment.* New York: Longman, 1984.

United States Commission on Civil Rights. *Window Dressing on the Set: A Report.* Washington, DC: Government Printing Office, 1977.

United States Commission on Civil Rights. *Window Dressing on the Set: An Update.* Washington, DC: Government Printing Office, 1979.

Wicklein, John. *Electronic Nightmare: The New Communications and Freedom.* New York: Viking, 1981.

Williams, Fred. *The Communications Revolution.* Rev. ed. New York: Mentor, 1983.

Wolf, Frank. *Television Programming for News and Public Affairs.* New York: Praeger, 1972.

Wright, John, ed. *The Commercial Connection: Advertising and the Mass Media.* New York: Dell, 1979.

Chapter 9
Television Criticism

OVERVIEW

Television has become such a pervasive part of our environment that one would be hard pressed to find many in the population of viewers and nonviewers who would not consider themselves "expert" in terms of cataloging the medium's perceived faults or virtues. The problem is that few really understand the fundamental nature of the medium, yet many are quick to give credence to the "familarity breeds contempt" platitude. Fortunately, criticism of the medium does not bunch up at one pole and end there; instead, it covers a broad-ranging continuum with ample room to accommodate a number of multilevel perspectives.

In this chapter, we attempt to cover a number of such perspectives, ranging from the popular "bad mouth" approach to the sophistication of the semiologist who uses an unfamiliar language to read the TV text. In a way, all approaches are valid and deserve our consideration. At the outset, however, we ask this question: "But what of standards and criteria for broadcasting criticism?" It has been pointed out that there is no agreed-upon set of principles and that the criteria that have been established can be considered only as starting points. We would be remiss if we did not also state the obvious: there is much work that needs to be done to give television criticism the tradition it does not now have.

CRITICISM: PRO AND CON

We found six titles that conveniently divide into the pro-TV and the anti-TV positions. Three of the most vitriolic of criticisms aimed at television were written by sociologist Rose Goldsen, ad man Jerry Mander, and academician Peter Conrad. In *The Show and Tell Ma-*

chine: How Television Works and Works You Over, Goldsen tackles the entire television industry with the passion of a crusader bent on single-handedly ridding the TV pollutants from our physical and psychic environments. She takes on the portrayal of family life on prime time and daytime drama, violence, news, laugh-tracks, the Nielsen ratings, and a host of other TV topics with essentially the same posture: television's power to manipulate mass consciousness is tyrannizing America and endangering the future.

Like Goldsen, Jerry Mander, in *Four Arguments for the Elimination of Television,* believes television to be nonreformable. He advocates the elimination of television for the following reasons: (1) TV creates an artificial environment which alienates the viewer from the real world; (2) TV caters to the interests of large corporations and not the average person; (3) TV causes neurophysiological dysfunctions (e.g., it hypnotizes the viewer); and (4) TV has a limited potential for improvement and change. Unfortunately, Mander's arguments are largely emotional, based upon assumptions that are suspect rather than upon research-derived data.

In *Television: The Medium and Its Manners,* Conrad does little more than complain about TV's duplicity, crassness, arrogance, and bad manners. Whether news or soap operas, talk shows or drama, advertising or game shows—even when TV is considered as nothing more than a silent piece of furniture—Conrad's harangue is all the same. There is nothing good to be said, nothing neutral.

Three titles taking a positive view are *Station Identification: Confessions of a Video Kid,* by Donald Bowie; *Television Viewers vs. Media Snobs: What TV Does for People,* by Jib Fowles; and *Demographic Vistas: Television in American Culture,* by David Marc. Bowie's volume is at once a video-biographical, historical, critical, and introspective experience as revealed by a member of the first television generation. Documenting one man's internalization of the television experience and relating the events in the real world to those in the television world, Bowie has touched a responsive chord in all videophiles. Fowles's book makes the claim that television has beneficial effects for its viewers: it is good for mental health because it relaxes the viewer after a hard day in the workplace; it is a catharsis or displacement for unacceptable social behavior; and its fantasy not only hugs the viewer with a warm security blanket but may vicariously transfer feelings of love, power, respect, and assertiveness. Rounding out this group of titles, David Marc's book takes a holistic, positive stance: he accepts the medium and its messages with unabashed respect, applying the tools of theatrical and literary criticism to justify his position.

UNDERSTANDING TELEVISION

Responsible critics, concerned as they are with evaluation, also bring to their work the explanation of the scientist, the truth of the mystic, and the argumentation of the rhetorician. The hoped-for result, if all goes as the critic plans, is to give the public new insights in order to assist them in making future decisions. Although, to some, helpful evaluations and useful insights constitute the greatest contribution a critic can make, the bottom line for others is to pursue a different commitment: reform, high standards, Marxism, praise of celebrities, protection of consumers, and promotion of understanding of the medium. All of this, in addition to pragmatic concerns that may be imposed by considerations of the interests and needs of the source or the audience, or by self-imposed ego concerns of reputation and status, makes the critic's assignment complex. However, the *sine qua non* of all critics is to be open-minded and fair as well as sensitive, analytical, knowledgeable, and creative and skillful in communicating their ideas and evaluations.

One of the most significant books in the development of broadcast criticism is Gilbert Seldes's 1950 publication *The Great Audience.* A historical/descriptive account of professional broadcasting criticism is supplied by Ralph Lewis Smith's 1959 Ph.D. dissertation, *A Study of the Professional Criticism of Broadcasting in the United States 1920–1955,* recently published as part of Arno Press's "Dissertations in Broadcasting" series. *On the Small Screen,* by Hal Himmelstein, and *Beyond the Wasteland,* by Robert Rutherford Smith are also excellent state-of-the-art publications. Martin Mayer's *About Television* covers a number of provocative themes, including children's programming, creative research, the potentially overrated view of communication technology as the great problem solver, and the question of political access.

Understanding Television, edited by Richard Adler, is an outgrowth of his two earlier compilations, *Television as a Social Force* and *Television as a Cultural Force* (with Douglass Cater), which are collections of conference papers. This expanded new edition, which dropped some of the earlier, less relevant material, is a critical study of television's institutional and programmatic aspects. In the same vein as the Adler anthologies, Horace Newcomb's *Television: The Critical View* presents a broad view of the television environment. The essays deal with critical analyses of program types, placing programs within a cultural context and attempting to define television in relation to itself as well as other mass media.

Taking still another perspective in the attempt to understand television, John Ravage, in *Television: The Director's Viewpoint,* presents a unique assessment of the major issues facing television as revealed in interviews with 12 of television's leading directors. One of Ravage's most penetrating statements appears in the first chapter, in which he describes the industry's deliberate, cliff-hanging manipulations to keep the mass audience captive so as to absorb the upcoming commercials. Laments Ravage, "Seldom are humans shown as they come to grips with real issues, or with themselves as fallible creatures, trying to understand the difficult questions life poses" (p. 10).

On the other hand, David Althiede and Robert Snow, in *Media Logic,* suggest that people equate what they experience on television as being representative of the real world. (Jerry Kosinski went one step further in *Being There* with his portrayal of Chance for whom the TV world *was* the real world.) Do people really expect medical practitioners in real life to have the bedside manners of television's Marcus Welby or Trapper John; the police in real life to have the ready solutions of Kojak, Columbo, and Ironside; and real-life families to have the insight and understanding of the Waltons, the Ingallses (*Little House on the Prairie*), and the Laurences (*Family*)? Is not the more approximate truth that television does not so much reflect society or human behavior as attempt to establish meanings?

The thesis of Ben Stein's *View from Sunset Boulevard* is that a few hundred Hollywood writers and producers are imposing their visions of the world upon the television public, with the danger that viewers may be deluded into thinking that the TV world is a reasonable facsimile of life off the screen. Critics such as Frank Mankiewicz and Joel Swerdlow argue in their book *Remote Control* that the "entertainmentizing" of serious social issues widens the gap between vicarious involvement and overt commitment to action; that while prime time television does give a great deal of coverage to such current social issues as the women's movement and minority rights, an overwhelming number of those uninvolved remain overwhelmingly uninvolved. According to Mankiewicz and Swerdlow, the very act of spending time watching the TV treatment of such subjects narcotizes women into a state of acceptance of their traditional role and place in society. Television, in using the ideal-norms concept in its approach to defining social issues and prescribing solutions to problems, can easily delude the viewer into believing that progress is being made and that all is well with the world.

What appears to be lacking in the literature of television criticism are works devoted to the analysis and evaluation of specific television program types. Two titles are cited here as appropriate overviews of program genres—Horace Newcomb's *TV: The Most Popular Art* and Hal Himmelstein's *Television Myth and the American Mind.* Newcomb analyzes popular television genres—situation comedies, westerns, mysteries, adventure shows, soap operas, and news shows—as art forms, positing that the very sense of intimacy, continuity, and history that so many television serials impart to the viewer may impose another barrier between the TV world and the real world, adding to the false sense of complacency that the viewer might so easily come to assume. Himmelstein's work is also organized around the various television genres, looking at structure and message—in terms of its manifest and latent content—to arrive at meaning.

David Grote studies the situation comedy in *The End of Comedy: The Sit-Com and the Comedic Tradition* from the perspective of traditional comedy history. Grote sees the situation comedy as the keeper of the status quo and theatrical comedy as the vehicle for social change.

Of the few critical appraisals of a specific program, Richard Adler's edited book, *All in the Family,* is outstanding. It brings together samplings of scripts, critical reviews, research studies, analytical essays, and a symposium setting forth the comments of critics and TV industry leaders. A listing of all the episodes in this series from 1971 through the 1978–1979 season, photographs of some of the more memorable scenes, and a bibliography of further readings make this an invaluable critical historical source book for one of television's most significant programs.

Another such work is *Thirty Seconds* by Michael Arlen. The essays in this book appeared originally in *The New Yorker,* but unlike Arlen's other compilations, this book concentrates on a single subject—the 30-second commercial. The essays trace the production of the commercial from conception through all its stages to final airing. The depth of detail that Arlen presents in this carefully constructed case history, coupled with his entertaining style of writing, makes this book appealing to both the general reader and the serious scholar.

Critical reviews of various individual television programs, of course, frequently appear in the TV section of the newspaper, *TV Guide,* or other magazines—some before the fact and many more afterwards, thereby not performing the service function of recommending the good and not recommending the bad, as a book reviewer or movie reviewer might do. For that reason, television critics often write more broadly about various aspects of the television industry, and afterwards, they compile their newspaper or magazine columns into book-length examinations of the television medium. Perhaps the most prolific is Michael Arlen, television critic for *The New Yorker. Thirty Seconds* has already been mentioned; *The Living Room War, The View from Highway I,* and *The Camera Age* are other samples of his work. Former *Saturday Review* critic Robert Lewis Shayon's *Open to Criticism,* Eugene Burdick's *The Eighth Art,* and Robert Sklar's *Prime-Time America* contain perceptive evaluations of the problems and potentials of the television industry.

READING TELEVISION

A new way of looking at television—semiology—has captured the interest of researchers on both sides of the Atlantic. Several titles are suggested here as alternative ways of analyzing the text of television. In her book, *The TV Ritual,* Gregor Goethals states the claim that Americans have shifted their need for spiritual significance from temples of worship to the altar of television. One of the earliest attempts to bring the cultural role of television into a symbiotic relationship with semiological analysis is found in John Fiske and John Hartley's *Reading Television,* in which the authors, critically reading specific television texts, illustrate the differences between TV realism and print realism. Two additional British titles, *The Message of Television,* by Roger Silverstone, and *The Language of Television,* by Albert Hunt, detail the problems that are encountered in semiological research.

ETHICAL ISSUES

As the media grow in complexity and importance, ethical issues in the media keep pace with ethical concerns of society. Harry Skornia deals with the question, How well does television fit into our society's institutional and social framework?, in *Television and Society: An Inquest and Agenda for Improvement.* Skornia examines such issues as the impact of the commercialization of broadcasting, governmental regulation, ratings, and America's image abroad. In *Ethics, Morality, and the Media,* edited by Lee Thayer, the subject of media ethics cuts across all the major mass media including public opinion polling, covering such aspects as news, entertainment, advertising, and public relations. Two titles, *Media Ethics: Cases and Moral Reasoning,* by Clifford Christians, Kim Rotzoll, and Mark Fackler, and *Philosophy and Journalism,* by John Merrill and S. Jack Odell, challenge the reader to examine his or her own standards of media performance in the areas of information, persuasion, and diversion through the presentation of a number of ethical quandaries in journalism, advertising, and entertainment.

Two additional titles, both by John Phelan, also tackle the problem of media moral dilemmas. *Disenchantment: Meaning and Morality in the Media* explores three major contexts of moral awareness in the mass media: (1) the method of functionalism, (2) the unholy alliance of censorship consumerism, and (3) technological determinism. In *Mediaworld: Programming the Public,* Phelan's concern is with the public's moral disarmament by the media.

Three classic titles are concerned with the successful, manipulative practices of advertising. Vance Packard's *Hidden Persuaders* looks at what motivational research is doing to us, while Wilson Bryan Key's two books, *Subliminal Seduction* and *Media Sexploitation* examine the hidden sexual messages in media advertising. Finally, Donna Woolfolk Cross's recent book, *Mediaspeak: How Television Makes up Your Mind,* reviews the way the media manipulate us emotionally and create a pseudoreality.

THE AUDIENCE TALKS BACK

Criticism cannot be successfully carried out without the willing complicity of the viewing public, who must first be made aware of the elements constituting "good" television. Representative of a number of books that have been written from the point of view of citizen pressure groups are Nicholas Johnson's *How to Talk Back to Your Television Set,* its sequel, *Test Pattern for Living,* and Les Brown's *Keeping Your Eye on Television.* They are essential reading for those citizens who would wish to assume a more active posture in decision making with regard to TV regulations.

Additionally, two books, *Television Awareness Training,* edited by Ben Logan and Kate Moody, and *Inside Television: A Guide to Critical Viewing,* by Ned White, offer complete self-help approaches to guide the viewer toward acquiring a deepening awareness of the television world and the real world. Both books cover a number of television's most controversial issues and offer workshop exercises and lists of additional readings.

BIBLIOGRAPHY

Adler, Richard, ed. *All in the Family: A Critical Appraisal.* New York: Praeger, 1979.

————. *Television as a Social Force: New Approaches to TV Criticism.* New York: Praeger, 1975.

————. *Understanding Television: Essays on Television as a Social and Cultural Force.* New York: Praeger, 1981.

Adler, Richard, and Cater, Douglass, eds. *Television as a Cultural Force.* New York: Praeger, 1976.

Altheide, David L., and Snow, Robert P. *Media Logic.* Beverly Hills, CA: Sage, 1979.

Arlen, Michael J. *The Camera Age: Essays on Television.* New York: Farrar, Straus & Giroux, 1981.

————. *The Living Room War.* New York: Viking, 1969.

————. *Thirty Seconds.* New York: Farrar, Straus & Giroux, 1980.

————. *View from Highway I: Essays on Television.* New York: Farrar, Straus & Giroux, 1976.

Bowie, Donald. *Station Identification: Confessions of a Video Kid.* New York: M. Evans, 1980.

Brown, Les. *Keeping Your Eye on Television.* New York: Pilgrim, 1979.

Burdick, Eugene, et al. *The Eighth Art: 23 Views of Television Today.* New York: Holt, Rinehart, and Winston, 1962.

Christians, Clifford G.; Rotzoll, Kim B.; and Fackler, Mark. *Media Ethics: Cases and Moral Reasoning.* New York: Longman, 1983.

Conrad, Peter. *Television: The Medium and Its Manners.* Boston, MA: Routledge & Keagan Paul, 1982.

Cross, Donna Woolfolk. *Mediaspeak: How Television Makes up Your Mind.* New York: New American Library, 1983.

Fiske, John, and Hartley, John. *Reading Television.* London: Metheun, 1978.

Fowles, Jib. *Television Viewers vs. Media Snobs: What TV Does for People.* New York: Stein & Day, 1982.

Goethals, Gregor T. *The TV Ritual: Worship at the Video Altar.* Boston: Beacon, 1981.

Goldsen, Rose K. *The Show and Tell Machine: How Television Works and Works You Over.* New York: Dial, 1977.

Grote, David. *The End of Comedy: The Sit-Com and the Comedic Tradition.* Hamden, CT: Shoe String Press, 1983.

Himmelstein, Hal. *On the Small Screen: New Approaches in Television and Video Criticism.* New York: Praeger, 1981.

———. *Television Myth and the American Mind.* New York: Praeger, 1984.

Hunt, Albert. *The Language of Television.* London: Eyre Methuen, 1981.

Johnson, Nicholas. *How to Talk Back to Your Television Set.* Boston: Little Brown, 1970.

———. *Test Pattern for Living.* New York: Bantam Books, 1972.

Key, Wilson Bryan. *Media Sexploitation.* Englewood Cliffs, NJ: Prentice-Hall, 1976.

———. *Subliminal Seduction.* Englewood Cliffs, NJ: Prentice-Hall, 1973.

Kosinski, Jerry. *Being There.* New York: Bantam Books, 1970.

Logan, Ben, and Moody, Kate, eds. *Television Awareness Training: The Viewer's Guide for Family and Community.* New York: Action Research Center, 1979.

Mander, Jerry. *Four Arguments for the Elimination of Television.* New York: Morrow, 1978.

Mankiewicz, Frank, and Swerdlow, Joel. *Remote Control: Television and the Manipulation of American Life.* New York: Ballantine Books, 1978.

Marc, David. *Demographic Vistas: Television in American Culture.* Philadelphia, PA: University of Pennsylvania Press, 1981.

Mayer, Martin. *About Television.* New York: Harper & Row, 1972.

Merrill, John C., and Odell, S. Jack. *Philosophy and Journalism.* New York: Longman, 1983.

Newcomb, Horace. *TV: The Most Popular Art.* New York: Oxford University Press, 1976.

Newcomb, Horace, ed. *Television: The Critical View.* New York: Oxford University Press, 1976. 2d ed., 1979.

Packard, Vance. *The Hidden Persuaders.* New York: David McKay, 1957.

Phelan, John M. *Disenchantment: Meaning and Morality in the Media.* New York: Hastings House, 1980.

———. *Mediaworld: Programming the Public.* New York: Seabury Press, 1977.

Ravage, John W. *Television: The Director's Viewpoint.* Boulder, CO: Westview, 1978.

Seldes, Gilbert Vivian. *The Great Audience.* New York: Viking, 1950.

Shayon, Robert Lewis. *Open to Criticism.* Boston: Beacon, 1971.

Silverstone, Roger. *The Message of Television.* London: Heinemann Educational Books, 1981.

Sklar, Robert. *Prime-Time America: Life on and behind the Television Screen.* New York: Oxford University Press, 1980.

Skornia, Harry J. *Television and Society: An Inquest and Agenda for Improvement.* New York: McGraw-Hill, 1965.

Smith, Ralph Lewis. *A Study of the Professional Criticism of Broadcasting in the United States, 1920–1953.* New York: Arno, 1979.

Smith, Robert Rutherford. *Beyond the Wasteland: The Criticism of Broadcasting.* Annandale, VA: Speech Communication Association; Urbana, IL: ERIC Clearing House on Reading and Communication Skills, 1976.

Stein, Benjamin. *The View from Sunset Boulevard: America as Brought to You by the People Who Make Television.* New York: Basic Books, 1979.

Thayer, Lee. *Ethics, Morality, and the Media.* New York: Hastings House, 1980.

Tunstall, Jeremy. *The Media Are America.* London: Constable, 1977; New York: Columbia University Press, 1977.

White, Ned. *Inside Television: A Guide to Critical Viewing.* Palo Alto, CA: Science and Behavior Books, 1980.

Chapter 10
Collected Works

OVERVIEW

This final chapter deals with selected collected works of mass communication, most of which have brought together a wide-ranging agenda of divergent perspectives. In placing most of our selections of collected works in this chapter (with the exception of those coinciding with the themes of earlier chapters), we eliminated the thorny problem of classification. The value in collected works is that they not only represent the "think pieces" of a divergent group of scholars, but they also give alternative perspectives of the perceived priorities, issues, problems, and concerns of the field.

It is also important to preserve some sense of the history of the progression and development of the critical pressure points in the field. Therefore, we have made an effort to present these works in some reasonable order of date of publication, unless the logic of thematic groupings justified we do otherwise.

EARLY ANTHOLOGIES

Among the earliest of the anthologies included here, Bernard Rosenberg and David Manning White's *Mass Culture: The Popular Arts in America* (1957) remains one of the most enduring books on the role of the mass media in society. The book draws upon scholars from various disciplines in an attempt to give the topic of mass culture, and ultimately the mass media, its first defined, systemized perspective. Even earlier, Schramm's pioneering first edition of *Mass Communications* (1949) attempted to bring together the diverse views of a prestigious cadre of scholars in such disciplines as anthropology, psychology, sociology, political science, and economics as well as scholars and professionals in the field of mass communication. Schramm's second edition (1960) highlights the phenomenal growth and development of television.

Several major anthologies, spanning the period from 1964 to 1972, take an in-depth look at the communication process from a sociological perspective. *People, Society, and Mass Communications* (1964) by Lewis Dexter and David Manning White is intended for mass media professionals, scholars, and students. This book explores the interplay between the communicator and audience, highlights the state of communication research, and critiques the bibliography of mass communication. Paul Halmos, editor of *The Sociology of the Mass-Media Communicators* (1969) attempts to correct an imbalance with regard to the study of the mass communication process by focusing on both the communicator and the recipient within the context of their group relationships and various affiliations and in terms of interaction and feedback—all within the larger social system. The Jeremy Tunstall reader *Media Sociology* (1970) contains the British preoccupation with the role of communication organizations and communicators. The 25 essays, two-thirds reprinted and one-third original, also examine the other components of the mass communication process, such as the interaction between content and audience and media and politics. Denis McQuail's anthology *Sociology of Mass Communications* (1972), while it is regrettably out of print, also deserves a place in a basic collection of books on mass communication for its carefully selected conceptual essays and its strong theoretical emphasis. Reflecting the author's sociology background, this book focuses on organizational and sociological settings, with selections exploring the relationship between the behavior of and the social context of the audience member. The inclusion of public policy essays from a number of different countries offers still another perspective for the student interested in the study of cross-cultural communication.

Two titles that should be considered together are the *Reader in Public Opinion and Communication* (1966), edited by Bernard Berelson and Morris Janowitz, and its renamed successor, *Reader in Public Opinion and Mass Communication* (1981), edited by Morris Janowitz and Paul Hirsch. Only six essays appear in both editions. The 1966 edition has 54 essays, at least 45 of which are still timely today; the 1981 edition has 35 essays, reflecting the "Mass Communication" perspective in its title by focusing more heavily on the mass media components. With a minimum of duplication, each edition contains the work of the most respected scholars and researchers in the field. The two editions should have been issued as companion volumes offering the student of public opinion and communication a valuable historical document, tracing the evolution of the field as well as well as providing a solid source of research and scholarship.

THE CRITICAL PERSPECTIVE

Two additional volumes should also be considered together because of similarity of subject matter. The first is *Media and Symbols: The Forms of Expression, Communication and Education* (1974), edited by David Olson, the seventy-third yearbook of the National Society for the Study of Education. The second is a more recent publication, *Popular Television and Film: A Reader* (1981), by Tony Bennett, Susan Boyd-Bowman, Colin Mercer, and Janet Woolacott. The Olson volume is divided into three sections: (1) "Media, Modes and Symbol Systems," (2) "The Educational Potential of Various Media," and (3) "Technology and Institutions." According to Olson, whose 18 authors acquitted themselves brilliantly, the goal was "to provide a general conceptualization of the nature of media and symbols that would reflect their important place in our conception of man and his culture and, at the same time, would indicate, if in a preliminary way, their uses and effects in the educational enterprise" (p. 10). According to the critics, this goal was met.

The Bennett anthology, which brings together 22 articles unified in content and style, examines the "text" of television and film through the application of concepts from structuralism, semiology, psychoanalysis, and politics. Divided into four parts, which favor television over film, the book covers genre, the discourses of television, popular film and the viewing experience, and history in the context of television.

Two volumes from Britain's Open University also command attention. The first publication, *Mass Communication and Society* (originally published in 1977 in Britain and 1979 in the United States), edited by James Curran, Michael Gurevitch, and Janet Woolacott, was reportedly assembled for a BBC-TV Open University course for which students might have difficulty obtaining access to library materials. It covers, at a rather sophisticated level, major perspectives on mass media and society, media organizations and occupations, and the interrelationship of the media and other cultural phenomena such as art and music.

The second title, *Culture, Society and the Media* (1982), edited by Michael Gurevitch, Tony Bennett, James Curran, and Janet Gurevitch, uses two theoretical frames—liberal-pluralist and Marxist—for each of its three sections into which the readings have been categorized: (1)

"Class, Ideology and the Media," (2) "Media Organization,"and (3) "The Power of the Media." The essays are well written, and perhaps this volume's most significant contribution lies in the variety of Marxist perspectives it offers the reader.

An appropriate link between the titles just discussed and mass communication perspectives in the United States and other countries is the volume *Communication and Social Structure: Critical Studies in Mass Media Research* (1981), edited by Emile McAnany, Jorge Schnitman, and Noreene Janus. The intent of this volume is to examine the research perspectives outside the mainstream of traditional U.S. research in order to better understand the relativity of our own approaches to communication problem solving.

PRAGMATIC PERSPECTIVES

On the American side of the Atlantic, we find a diverse set of pragmatic perspectives. For example, *The New Languages* (1977), edited by Thomas Olhgren and Lynn Berk, suggests two approaches to the study of the mass media: (1) understanding the media environment and (2) understanding the basic concepts of rhetoric. Because of the second approach, this is a useful book for writing and speech courses.

Beyond Media (1979), edited by Richard Budd and Brent Ruben, is an attempt to redefine the concept of mass communication. The intent of the book is to broaden our view of what actually constitutes mass communication. Aside from the traditional radio-TV-newspaper media, the authors argue for the inclusion of such elements as architecture, religion, popular art, museums, and libraries. The editors explain that they are attempting to "establish the notion that mass communication is a broad phenomenon which is communicationally indigenous to all social organizations, and that the number of institutions seving that function in our society is far greater than here-to-fore recognized" (preface).

Manfred Meyer, in *Health Education by Television and Radio: Contributions to an International Conference with a Selected Bibliography* (1981), brings together a broad spectrum of the conference's contributors including health educators, communication researchers, journalists, and PR experts and broadcast editors involved in health education programs. Exploring the matter of the mass media's effectiveness in communicating health education messages to influence behavior, the importance of the conference and this volume underscores the productive use of broadcasting media for purposes other than entertainment.

THE CONTINUING DEBATE

A number of readers have raised questions about and debate the fundamental issues in mass communication. While these readers have assumed many forms—debates, commentary, the absence of commentary—the significance of these books is that they do focus on the most important issues, and these issues have remained fundamentally the same. The selections in Harry Skornia and Jack Kitson's *Problems and Controversies in Television and Radio* (1968) were chosen not for their recentness but for their timelessness and general unavailability. The previously unpublished position statements of broadcasting's opinion leaders, out-of-print historical pieces, and other basic documents of the industry reposing in archival files present adequate starting points for discussion and debate for seminar courses on broadcasting's more enduring problems and issues.

Nearly fifteen years after the Skornia book, George McKenna's edited volume, *Media Voices: Debating Critical Issues in Mass Media* (1982) appeared, without missing a beat. Presenting many of the same issues and controversies debated by its predecessor, McKenna invited prominent media scholars and practitioners to voice their positions on such issues as media regulations, the concentration of media ownership, and violence.

Three other titles, which are strong enough to serve as the sole texts for introductory courses on mass media, are Francis Voelker and Ludmila Voelker, *Mass Media: Forces in Our Society* (1978); Everette Dennis, Arnold Ismach, and Donald Gillmor, *Enduring Issues in Mass Communication* (1978); and George Rodman, *Mass Media Issues: Analysis and Debate* (1981). Anthologies such as these are selected as supplemental readings in more advanced mass communication courses dealing with controversy and current problems.

Another title that should not be overlooked is Barry Cole's *Television Today: A Close-Up View* (1981). From a bank of 11,000 articles that have appeared in *TV Guide* since its inception, Cole has selected 64, written introductions for them, updated them where necessary, providing us with an overview of television programming. He covers such aspects as programming, audience, regulations, TV's significance in today's society, and its future.

ANNUAL REVIEWS

Two yearbook series, which in recent years have graced the communication research scene, are attempting to deal with the vast literature of the field to assist communication research scholars in keeping abreast of current developments and emphases. The International Communication Association has already issued the eighth volume of its *Communication Yearbook* series, the format of which consists of topical disciplinary reviews and commentaries, state-of-the-art overviews of the subdivisions within the broad field of communication (e.g., Information Systems, Intercultural Communication, Mass Communication, Political Communication), and representative research carried out during the year. The series, *Mass Communication Review Yearbook,* focuses on the research in the field of mass communication alone. Now in its fourth year, this series, which is international in scope, attempts to synthesize ongoing work that charts new directions as well as to encourage collaborative efforts among scholars from various parts of the world.

BIBLIOGRAPHY

Bennett, Tony, et al. *Popular Television and Film: A Reader.* London: British Film Institute, 1981.

Berelson, Bernard, and Janowitz, Morris, eds. *Reader in Public Opinion and Communication.* 2d ed. New York: Free Press, 1966.

Budd, Richard W., and Ruben, Brent D. *Beyond Media: New Approaches to Mass Communication.* Rochelle Park, NJ: Hayden Press, 1978.

Cole, Barry G., ed. *Television Today. A Close-Up View: Readings from TV Guide.* New York: Oxford University Press, 1981.

Curran, James; Gurevitch, Michael; and Woolacott, Janet. *Mass Communication and Society.* Beverly Hills, CA: Sage, 1979.

Dennis, Everette E.; Ismach, Arnold H.; and Gillmor, Donald M., eds. *Enduring Issues in Mass Communication.* St. Paul, MN: West, 1978.

Dexter, Lewis Anthony, and White, David Manning, eds. *People, Society, and Mass Communications.* New York: Free Press, 1964.

Gurevitch, Michael, et al., eds. *Culture, Society, and the Media.* New York: Methuen, 1982.

Halmos, Paul, ed. *The Sociology of the Mass-Media Communicators.* Keele, Staffordshire, UK: University of Keele, 1969.

International Communication Association. *Communication Yearbook.* Vol 1-, New Brunswick, NJ: Transaction Books, 1977–.

Janowitz, Morris, and Hirsch, Paul, eds. *Reader in Public Opinion and Mass Communication.* 3d ed. New York: Free Press, 1981.

Mass Communication Review Yearbook. Beverly Hills, CA: Sage, 1980–.

McAnany, Emile G.; Schnitman, Jorge; and Janus, Noreene, eds. *Communication and Social Structure: Critical Studies in Mass Research.* Grass Valley, CA: Cambria Press, 1981.

McKenna, George, ed. *Media Voices: Debating Critical Issues in Mass Media.* Guilford, CT: Dushkin, 1982.

McQuail, Denis. *Sociology of Mass Communications: Selected Readings.* New York: Penguin, 1972.

Meyer, Manfred, ed. *Health Education by Television and Radio.* New York and Munich: K.G. Sauer, 1981.

Ohlgren, Thomas, and Berk, Lynn M., eds. *The New Languages: A Rhetorical Approach to the Mass Media and Popular Culture.* Englewood Cliffs, NJ: Prentice-Hall, 1977.

Olson, David R., ed. *Media and Symbols: The Forms of Expression, Communications, and Education.* The Seventy-Third Yearbook of the National Society for the Study of Education. Chicago: University of Chicago Press, 1974.

Rodman, George, ed. *Mass Media Issues: Analysis and Debate.* Chicago: Science Research Associates, 1981.

Rosenberg, Bernard, and White, David Manning, eds. *Mass Culture: The Popular Arts in America.* New York: Free Press, 1957.

Schramm, Wilbur Lang, ed. *Mass Communications: A Book of Readings.* 2d ed. Urbana, IL: University of Illinois Press, 1960.

Skornia, Harry Jay, and Kitson, Jack William. *Problems and Controversies in Television and Radio: Basic Readings.* Palo Alto, CA: Pacific Books, 1968.

Tunstall, Jeremy, ed. *Media Sociology: A Reader.* Urbana, IL: University of Illinois Press, 1970.

Voelker, Francis H., and Voelker, Ludmila A. *Mass Media: Forces in Our Society.* 3d ed. San Diego, CA: Harcourt, Brace, Jovanovich, 1978.

Afterword

It is fitting to conclude this guide with the citation of the *Journal of Communication's* unique volume, *Ferment in the Field* (Summer 1983), a compilation of 35 original essays on the state of communication research today.* Noting that it has been nearly a quarter century ago since Bernard Berelson eulogized the field in his now famous "the State of Communication Research," the editors of the *Ferment* volume, George Gerbner and Marsha Siefert, charged their invited contributors to speak to "the state of communications research today: the relationship of the researcher to science, society and policy; the goals of research with respect to social issues and social structure; and the tactics and strategies for reaching their goals" (p. 4). The contributors' responses to this charge confirmed the basic notion that ferment revitalizes the soul of our discipline and illuminates the road yet to be traveled.

As a final note, it is our belief that we have barely scratched the surface in covering the vast literature of television. So pervasive a medium demands continuous study, which in turn will continue to add to the already embarrassingly rich store of published materials on this subject. Even as we write this, we realize that not only is our work instantly outdated but that we have doubtlessly overlooked materials that should have been included. If we were dealing with a different subject and a different medium, we might feel uneasy, but because it is the nature of the medium to be voracious in its consumption of content, which in turn stimulates the endless study and debate of the process, we sense a certain vindication. For in the forward-looking hope of Gilbert Seldes, "Television's true literature has, in fact, yet to be written."

*George Gerbner and Marsha Siefert, eds., *Ferment in the Field* (Philadelphia, PA: Annenberg School Press, 1983).

Indexes

Author Index

Compiled by Fred Ramey

Title Index

Subject Index